Novel Bondage

Novel Bondage

*Slavery, Marriage, and Freedom
in Nineteenth-Century America*

TESS CHAKKALAKAL

University of Illinois Press
URBANA, CHICAGO, AND SPRINGFIELD

Library of Congress Cataloging-in-Publication Data
Chakkalakal, Tess.
Novel bondage : slavery, marriage, and freedom
in nineteenth-century America / Tess Chakkalakal.
    p.   cm.
Includes bibliographical references and index.
ISBN 978-0-252-03633-0 (cloth : alk. paper)
1. Slavery in literature.
2. Marriage in literature.
3. Slaves—United States—Social conditions.
4. African Americans in literature.
I. Title.
PS217.S55C45   2011
813'.3093543—dc22   2011008194

Contents

Acknowledgments   vii

Introduction: The Slave-Marriage Plot   1

1. Between Fiction and Experience:
    William Wells Brown's *Clotel*   15

2. *Dred* and the Freedom of Marriage:
    Harriet Beecher Stowe's Fiction of Law   31

3. Free, Black, and Married: Frank J. Webb's
    The Garies and Their Friends   47

4. "A Legally Unmarried Race": Frances Harper's
    Marital Mission   64

5. Wedded to Race: Charles Chesnutt's
    Stories of the Color Line   83

    Conclusion: Reading Hannah Crafts
    in the Twenty-First Century   107

    Notes   113

    Selected Bibliography   133

    Index   139

Acknowledgments

This project first took shape at Williams College. Allison Case, Theo Davis, John Kleiner, Gretchen Long, and Carol Ockman provided crucial feedback in the early stages of the project. It was during my brief, but enormously fruitful, time at Bowling Green State University where the project transformed into a book. This transition was due, in large part, to Timothy Messer-Kreuse who provided much needed encouragement and critique. Here at Bowdoin College, I have been fortunate to experience the intellectual generosity of members of the English department and the Africana Studies Program that enabled its completion. In particular, I would like to thank Marilyn Reizbaum, without whom I'd be lost. Sean Keilen deserves special mention for his willingness to talk with me about something he knows nothing about and for helping me to make the work cohere. I would like to thank Tamara Berger, Maria Giulia Fabi, and Ken Warren for taking the time to read these chapters with such care and intelligence. Finally, I would like to thank Stephen Meardon for his constant support and affection.

A slightly different version of chapter 5 appeared in *Representing Segregation: Toward an Aesthetics of Living Jim Crow, and Other Forms of Racial Division.* Eds. Brian Norman and Piper Kendrix Williams. Albany: SUNY Press, 2010.

Novel Bondage

Introduction

The Slave-Marriage Plot

A slave marrying according to law is a thing
unknown in the history of American slavery.
—Henry Bibb (1849)

What is a "slave-marriage" and what relationship does it bear to a legal marriage? Hidden from law and subject to separation, a slave-marriage was considered in nineteenth-century America to be so far outside the purview of legal forms of marriage that it seemed hardly worth mentioning. Lacking the legal capacity for matrimony, marriage for slaves, as Henry Bibb asserts in his 1849 slave narrative, "is a thing unknown in the history of American slavery."[1] But that is not to say, as Bibb's own marriage to Malinda proves, that slaves did not marry. As a number of slave testimonies and cases heard after the abolition of slavery suggest, slaves married in spite of the law that stipulated "the slave could not marry because he was legally incapable to consent, because the relation of husband and wife was inconsistent with that of master and slave."[2] Efforts to legalize slave-marriages following emancipation suggest that their marriages were, in fact, just as valued as legal marriages even though they were performed, originally, without legal sanction. Performed without the law, the slave-marriage was a figment of the slave's imagination inscribed in the form of fiction—but a fiction, as the following chapters reveal, with very real effects.

Novel Bondage examines the form of slave-marriages through a reading of nineteenth-century novels and short stories that inscribed their occurrence and describes how these nonlegal unions challenged what it meant to be husband and wife in nineteenth-century America. This book thus has several goals. It begins to fill a long-standing gap in our knowledge about the slave-marriage and the function it performed in political debates regarding slavery and emancipation. In particular, it examines the ways in which fictional accounts of slave-marriage were understood by the law, and it demonstrates how both the form of these fictions and readers' responses to them were implicated in ongoing debates about the nature, purpose, and law of marriage.

Without the law on their side, slave-marriages varied widely in how they were performed. Some slaves married for love; others were joined, often against the wishes of one or both of the marrying couple, for the purposes of multiplying a slaveholder's assets, while others resisted marriage altogether, fearing that marriage would make escape virtually impossible.[3] Unlike a legal marriage in which marriage altered the status of those entering into the institution, marriage did not change the condition of a slave. Slaves were slaves for life, but their marriages were not. A slave-marriage could be dissolved at any time, by sale or gift. The fact that slave law did not recognize marriages formed by slaves was a central, but often neglected, feature of arguments against slavery.

Being denied the right to marry, as William Wells Brown explains in his 1853 novel, *Clotel; or, The President's Daughter: A Narrative of Slave Life in the United States*, makes slavery not only an economic problem of labor but also an affective problem of intimacy: "Not content with depriving them of all the higher and holier enjoyments of this relation, by degrading and darkening their souls, the slaveholder denies to his victim even that slight alleviation of his misery, which would result from the marriage relation being protected by law and public opinion."[4] Contrary to the well-known feminist critique of legal marriage that viewed the slave and the wife as one, Brown argues that legal marriage has the power to actually alleviate the condition of the slave. Compared with the preeminent rights that slaves were denied—the right to vote and to own their bodies and labor—the denial of their right to marry was of less transcendent, yet more immediate, importance.

Although Brown's novel uses the denial of marriage as the basis for its antislavery argument, it is a novel preoccupied by the singularity of the slave's relationship to marriage: "[M]arriage . . . is a matter which the slaveholders do not think is of any importance, or of any binding force with their slaves; yet it would be doing that degraded class an injustice, not to acknowledge that many of them do regard it as a sacred obligation, and show a willingness to obey the commands of God on this subject."[5] Brown's disquisition on marriage begins by suggesting that the absence of legal marriage among slaves "degrades" and "darkens" their souls; he concludes by reporting that "many of them" rely upon what we might call a "higher law" to regulate their marriages.[6] Brown presents slave-marriage, at least in his fiction, as being superior to legal marriage because it has the power to transcend slave law and the false authority of slaveholders. Brown's fictional conception of slave-marriage is informed not only by his personal experiences as a slave but also by his reading of sentimental fiction. Alluding explicitly to Lydia Maria Child's short stories about the lasciviousness of slaveholders and the sexual abuse female slaves were forced to endure, Brown's antislavery position relied on the sentimental discourse of marriage in crucial ways.[7] Following from a detailed study of the role marriage plays in Brown's life and fiction, *Novel Bondage* explores works by Harriet Beecher Stowe, Frank J. Webb, Frances E. W. Harper, and Charles W. Chesnutt to locate the form and function of the slave-marriage in both the antislavery imagination and visions of Reconstruction.

◻ ◻ ◻

In nineteenth-century America, marriage was understood primarily in terms of a legal contract between a consenting man and woman. Slaves could not marry because they were legally incapable of giving consent, because the relation of husband and wife was inconsistent with that of master and slave, and because the slave had no status as a person before the law. Given slaves' status outside the law, the slave-marriage exists as an oxymoron: It connotes a relationship between a man and woman who were "married yet not married."[8] The hyphen is intended here to distinguish syntactically the peculiar form of the slave-marriage from the legal form of marriage. Understanding the divergence between these forms of marriage uncovers the intimate connection between slavery and marriage that has, for the most part, been cast in entirely pejorative terms.[9] As these chapters reveal, the histories of marriage, slavery, and freedom are deeply intertwined in the United States.

Although a slave-marriage joined those who were unable to form a legal marital contract, their exclusion from the legal aspects of marriage exemplifies what legal theorists call the "nonlegal domains of marital meaning and marital experience."[10] Drucilla Cornell has productively named this "the imaginary domain," a category that provides us with the necessary language to speak about these nonlegal relationships more formally.[11] Nineteenth-century fictions position slave-marriage, performed without legal sanction, as a less strategic, more intensely religious, and more intimate form of marriage than those bound by the law. Since most histories of marriage focus on the law and its effect on social and intimate relations, little attention has been paid to the ways in which slave-marriage shaped conceptions of nineteenth-century marriage practices.[12] Slave-marriages were represented in both slave narratives and slave fictions throughout the nineteenth century, but how to incorporate these sources into the history of slavery and marriage remains the subject of considerable critical debate. Echoing Brown's antislavery arguments, several historians of slavery have recently argued that the love and affection holding slave spouses together was more powerful than the contractual bonds of legal marriage. According to historical accounts, marriage between slaves "served as a means of resistance against oppression" and "was an anchor and a positive reference point for the enslaved, ultimately enabling them to survive the regime."[13] In other words, a slave-marriage was about the love between a man and a woman, and more: It also functioned as a form of nonviolent or passive resistance against the all-powerful, legalized system of slavery. That slave rebellion would be conceived in the form of marriage was formulated and circulated through nineteenth-century slave fictions rather than actual slave experience.

Yet much of what we know about slave-marriages today is the result of rigorous and often controversial historical inquiry conducted in the mid-twentieth century by pathbreaking social historians like John Blassingame, Charles Joyner, Herbert Gutman, Eugene Genovese, Elizabeth Fox-Genovese, and Deborah G. White, whose investigations of "the slave's inner life" from multiple perspectives, using nontraditional historical methods, effectively rewrote the history of American slavery from the perspective of the slave.[14] Relying largely upon personal records left by slaves, either in the form of written autobiography or oral testimony, historians have uncovered a broad swath of data that reveals the nature of intimacy among slaves.

Still, one of the most troubling features of slave intimacy, for the historian, is the lack of quantifiable data. The absence of numbers has led historians of slavery to rely increasingly upon stories about or by slaves. In her compelling history of sex between white women and black men in the nineteenth-century American South, Martha Hodes explains how her historical research led her dangerously close to writing fiction: "I found shards and bones, parts of conversations, and laconic responses to frightening questions. Sometimes I wondered, why not write a work of fiction on the same subject? Why was I compelled to write history—to tell not just a story, but a true story?"[15] Hodes's self-interrogation raises a number of important issues regarding the tensions between historical and fictional accounts of slavery. Hodes's desire to tell a true story about "illicit sex" echoes the antislavery impulse, as Frederick Douglass complains in his 1855 autobiography of the constraints placed upon his own political speeches and lectures, to "have the facts."[16]

At the same time, however, Hodes's commitment to drawing a distinction between historical and fictional accounts of intimate relations during slavery speaks to twentieth-century fictional accounts of slavery that fall under the category of "the neo-slave narrative."[17] Unlike these twentieth-century stories of slavery, often written from the perspective of the slave, Hodes's history of intimate relations "is not a timeless phenomenon in the United States; rather it is a historical development that evolved out of particular social, political and economic circumstances. . . . [and that] complicates modern assumptions"[18] about slavery, assumptions that diminish the very real differences between how race operated in the nineteenth century and how it operates now. Despite her claims against writing history as fiction, the difficulty of gathering documentary evidence to support her history leads Hodes to delve into fictional territory nonetheless. I would like to suggest that rather than reject fiction, as Hodes does at the outset of her history, it might make more sense to probe nineteenth-century literary forms, particularly slave fiction, that are set amidst the particular social, political, and economic circumstances during which slave-marriages were performed and debated.

The historian's commitment to uncovering the truth about slavery, as Hodes and other historians have shown, requires us to rethink how we read nineteenth-century fiction. Since much of the history of slavery was undocumented, fiction has come to play an increasingly vital role in articulating the history of slavery. But how we read and evaluate that fiction remains an open question. Critics have responded to the status of these slave fictions, which often fall outside conventional literary categories, in a number of ways. Here I take up the work of John Ernest, whose work on nineteenth-century African American fiction and historiography has been crucial in bringing together the study of literature and history within African American studies. Given the importance of fiction to articulating the history of slavery, Ernest suggests that we rethink the concept of history itself. Rather than think of the history of slavery as an "all-powerful, monolithic" narrative, "it is important to think of history as something indicated by the mode of historical writing rather than as a story captured in a historical narrative."[19] Drawing from liberation theology's understanding of how oppression structures communities, Ernest invites us to read nineteenth-century African American history as a search "for a conception of a collective African American identity."[20] Arguing that this identity was forged in the interstices of conventional history and lived experience, Ernest describes how African American history was directed by its objective to create bonds between individuals who had experienced oppression, particularly in the form of slavery.

Although slave-marriage makes no appearance in Ernest's consideration of African American historical thought, it plays a crucial role in shaping the interventionist function of African American history that he describes as "a performative historiographical mode that supports the shifting performance of individual and collective African American identity necessitated by the containment of blackness within white nationalist history."[21] The slave-marriage offers a particularly poignant example of this "performative historiographical mode." Positioned outside conventional forms of literary and nonliterary discourse, the marital bond formed by slaves gained meaning and political value through particular works of nineteenth-century fiction. These works took aim not only at the familiar "horrors of slavery" but also at legal conventions of marriage in nineteenth-century America.

Several recent histories of marriage focus on nineteenth-century debates over the question of coverture, a legal doctrine that was almost always equated with slavery.[22] Like slavery, so the argument against coverture goes, a wife was made into the slave of her husband because all her property was transferred to her husband at the time of the marriage. The doctrine of coverture perverted, its critics argued, the idea of marriage. Lydia Maria Child and Sarah Grimké, both prominent abolitionists, each published books in the 1830s examining the history and condition of women worldwide, noting the many cultures in which wives were equated with property or slaves.[23] But imagining a different form of marriage, an alternative to legal marriage, was no simple task. The frequently drawn parallel between wives and slaves seemed, in fact, to change the condition of the slave, or at least to change how slave-marriages were viewed. As a marital relation that had little to do with either property or power, the slave-marriage came to embody the principles of an ideal marriage, a union of souls that transcended the earthly concerns upon which legal marriage was based.

It is perhaps not surprising that Child imagined what she considered to be ideal, equitable marriages in the form of her fiction rather than her nonfiction. Child's 1843 short story, "Slavery's Pleasant Homes, A Faithful Sketch," illustrates most explicitly the benefits of a slave-marriage over a legal one.[24] Considered a "buried masterpiece" within her literary corpus, Child's story provides one of the first fictional accounts of a slave-marriage that, as Carolyn L. Karcher has shown, was important to establishing the principles of antislavery fiction.[25] Departing in crucial ways from her antislavery manifesto published a decade earlier, Child's short story is less interested in presenting readers with the hard facts of slavery than with providing a real story—"A Faithful Sketch"—about slaves themselves.

The story recounts the life and death of two slaves—George and Rosa—who fall in love and marry shortly after George's master brings home his young bride. Set against the "dancing, shouting, clapping of hands, and eager invocations" that greet the newly married "massa and missis" is the slaves' courtship and marriage that "passed unnoticed."[26] As much as it is an indictment of the pain and suffering slavery inflicts upon the bodies of women, Child's story also inscribes and thereby lends legitimacy to the love between slaves. Like the more familiar story of Sethe's marriage to Halle in Toni Morrison's popular twentieth-century novel *Beloved* (1986), Child's story recognized the impossible situation of the slave husband. Whereas Halle is driven mad by witnessing the rape of his slave wife in Morrison's novel, George (in Child's story) keeps his wits, avenging the crimes committed against Rosa by murdering their master, Fredric Dalcho. George's actions are justified, Child argues, because Dalcho must be punished for violating both his own marriage and George and Rosa's slave-marriage.

More than mere tragedy, Child's "Sketch" is organized around a series of speech acts. The "eager invocations of blessing" that open the story are merely self-serving gestures that have little to do with celebrating the master's marriage and more to do with who would "get the largest coin, or the brightest handkerchief." Compared to this very public display of false affection, the "low talks among the rose-bushes, and stolen meetings by moonlight" between George and Rosa take on a more authentic character. Although witnessed only by "the silent presence of the stars," George and Rosa's slave-marriage "spoke whole volumes of mutual, happy love." The power of this *silent* love to *speak* volumes eventually drives Fredric Dalcho mad with lust and jealousy, leading him to rape and kill Rosa. To seek revenge and justice, her slave husband murders their master and is executed when he confesses to his crime of passion. Finally, the crime is "announced" in the newspaper, but the announcement, like the marriage "blessing" with which the story begins, proves false: This announcement distorts the truth about slavery by neglecting the needs and desires of the slave and, just as importantly, the master's criminal behavior. Relating the incidents wholly from the perspective of the slave owner and without consulting the slave's testimony, the newspapers declare Fredric Dalcho's innocence and the slave guilty of "*fiend-like murder*." Departing from these false accounts of relations between slaves and masters, Child's fiction presents readers with the story that "not one was found to tell" and "not one recorded." Not only does Child's story perform history by providing the untold and unrecorded story of slavery in the form of fiction, but it also gives voice to the slave's "silent" love. Telling the *true* story of slavery, in Child's terms, relies on fiction because there was no room in historical narratives of her time to account for the unspeakable crimes inflicted against slaves.[27] But the story is more than a history of slavery; it is also a story of true love.

"Why does the slave ever love?" Linda Brent, the narrator of Harriet Jacobs's 1861 slave narrative, *Incidents in the Life of a Slave Girl*, asks. "Why allow the tendrils of the heart to twine around objects which may at any moment be wrenched away by the hand of violence?"[28] The implication of Jacobs's slave narrative that "ends with freedom, not in the usual way, with marriage," is that slaves who fall in love are doomed to tragedy.[29] At least this is what happens to her. Brent, like Rosa and George, knows that, as a slave, she is not free to love and enjoy the pleasures and perils of romantic love. Yet, like George and Rosa, she does engage in the sexual and textual conventions of courtship and marriage, despite knowing that her courtship will not lead her to the happily-ever-after ending promised by the marriage plot. These tragic love stories manifest the problem of slavery, the ways in which slavery perverts the institution of marriage and disrupts the happy story of the marriage plot. But Child's story, unlike Jacobs's slave narrative of a fictional slave-marriage, does more than that. Because Child's slaves do marry, and risk their lives to do so, their love proves more "faithful" than that of the legal marriage between the master and his "delicate," "white" bride. Child's story begins with a sketch of a bad legal marriage and ends by celebrating those slaves who give up their lives to protect the *true* principles of marriage: "Not one was found to tell how the slave's young wife had been torn from him by his own brother, and murdered with slow tortures. Not one recorded the heroism that would not purchase life by another's death, though the victim was his enemy." Murdering his master in order to avenge the rape and death of his wife, and confessing to it, performs the legitimacy of the slave-marriage in fiction even though it lacks legal protection in reality.

Understanding the role of the slave-marriage in antislavery rhetoric and the discourse of emancipation requires a consideration of how what Ann duCille calls its "unreal estate" challenged the legal conventions of *both* slavery and marriage.[30] Although historians of slave culture have documented the importance of marriage to the formation of what Blassingame calls "the slave community,"[31] these accounts say little about how representations of slave-marriages challenged legal marriage and the inequality between the sexes that nineteenth-century marital laws enforced. Operating both outside and against the law, marriages formed by slaves offer a kind of fictional model for reforming marriage laws that enforced an unequal relation between husband and wife.

The most famous example of a slave-marriage was not, however, a fictional one. The sensational story of the marriage and escape of William and Ellen Craft from slavery captivated audiences during the mid-nineteenth century. Unlike most slave-marriages that were disrupted by involuntary separation or death, their marriage manifests a remarkable endurance against overwhelming odds. Their widely celebrated escape was essential to the antislavery plots of novels by both Harriet Beecher Stowe and Brown well before the Crafts' true version appeared in print in 1860. In Stowe's *Uncle Tom's Cabin* (1852), the Crafts are subsumed in the figures of George and

Eliza Harris. Although Stowe makes no explicit mention of the Crafts in the course of her fiction, she does call attention to the marriage between the slaves and uses their desire to protect their marriage as the primary motive for their escape. Eliza, after listening to her husband's lengthy diatribe about the injustices of slavery and the cruelties of his master, "trembled, and was silent."[32] Although she sympathizes with George's plight, she believes that she must obey her master and mistress in order to be a good Christian. It is only when George explains to her that his master plans to dissolve their marriage in order to marry him to another woman that Eliza is moved to take action. That is to say, it is only when their marriage is threatened that George is able to make Eliza understand the true nature of slavery: "Don't you know a slave can't be married? There is no law in this country for that; I can't hold you for my wife if he chooses to part us."[33] To preserve their marriage, George must run away with the expectation that Eliza will follow him so that they can continue to live "as if" they are husband and wife. Echoing the story of the Crafts' slave-marriage, Stowe's fictional characters illustrate the risks that slaves were willing to take in order to protect their marriage from the law.

The preeminent role marriage plays in Brown's and Stowe's antislavery fiction allows us to unravel the paradox underlying slave-marriage—a paradox that lies at the heart of legal marriage as well. Like William and Ellen Craft, George and Eliza Harris must escape from slavery if they are to protect the sanctity of their marital union. Since the law offers the couple no protection from being involuntarily separated, the slaves are willing to risk their lives in order to avoid being separated. According to Lydia Maria Child's version of the Crafts' marriage, "they were desirous to have their [marriage] ceremony performed again, with all the forms of law, now that they were in a free land."[34] Interestingly, William Craft makes no mention of the wedding ceremony in his version of their escape. In other words, the Crafts may have been "Running a Thousand Miles for Freedom," as the title to their 1860 narrative suggests, but what they found at the end of their very long and dangerous journey was a freedom contingent upon their right to be legally married. In the end, what made the story of William and Ellen Craft's escape from slavery so compelling for writers like Child, Stowe, and Brown was not just the transgressive means of their escape. It was their status as a *married* slave couple that made them into an instant sensation, a couple who affirmed the primacy of marriage and took considerable risks to protect their marriage from slave law. Each of the following chapters examines the ways in which the idea of the slave-marriage contributes to the social and political discourse of marriage in the United States.

Chapter 1, "Between Fiction and Experience: William Wells Brown's *Clotel*," reads Brown's preoccupation with marriage through both his fictional and autobiographical accounts of slavery. Generally believed to be the first novel by an African American, Brown's *Clotel; or, The President's Daughter* continues to be the subject of considerable critical controversy and debate.[35] Of course, the source of the novel's controversy rests not on marriage but rather on its absence. Purporting to tell the stories of Thomas Jefferson's slave mistress, daughters, and granddaughters, *Clotel* provides one of the earliest fictional accounts of the now scientifically verified conjugal relationship between the nation's founding father Thomas Jefferson and his slave Sally Hemings. Moving from this scandalous piece of the nation's history, Brown's romance provides something of an antidote to history. Relying, in part, on the lessons of Brown's own marriages—his first unconventional marriage to Elizabeth Schooner that ended in a personal scandal and his second, more conventional marriage to Annie Elizabeth Gray—my reading of his fiction rests on the disjunction between his autobiographical and fictional accounts of slave-marriage.

Chapter 2 examines the marriage plots running through Stowe's antislavery trilogy. Relying on the slave-marriage between George and Eliza, *Uncle Tom's Cabin* establishes two distinct marital categories: legal and nonlegal. Reading the opposition between slave and legal marriage plots in her subsequent antislavery novels, *Dred: A Tale of the Great Dismal Swamp* (1856) and *The Minister's Wooing* (1859), I examine the ways in which Stowe's novels posit the slave-marriage as a method of reforming conventional religious-legal marriage. Wedding her argument against slavery to her critique of marriage, Stowe aligns her antislavery principles with her proto-feminist ideas. Focusing on *Dred*'s romantic subplots, I examine the ways in which Stowe's antislavery fiction positions the slave-marriage as a literary ideal, one that its free white characters rely upon in making their own marital decisions. The juxtaposition between legal marriages and slave-marriages in the novel serves to interrogate the analogy between slavery and marriage that was highlighted by women's rights advocates of the period.

The importance of marriage to the formation of a *free* black antebellum community is the subject of the third chapter, "Free, Black, and Married: Frank J. Webb's *The Garies and Their Friends*." Webb's 1857 novel, *The Garies and Their Friends*, depicts the trials and tribulations of the growing free, black middle class of Philadelphia of which he and his first wife, the distinguished performer Mary E. Webb, were prominent members. Drawing upon Stowe's concept of the nonlegal slave-marriage as offering a more equitable and fruitful relationship between a husband and wife than the proprietary terms of a legal marriage, Webb's novel develops the terms of a free black marriage. Like Brown's, Webb's fiction reveals a consistent preoccupation with the subject of marriage. But unlike Brown, Webb distances his fiction from the law, as his novel recounts the marriage between a slave and her owner that is destroyed only after it is legalized in the North. Moving away from the legal rhetoric of marriage, *The Garies and Their Friends* imagines marriage—based perhaps on the author's own exemplary marriage—as an equal exchange between husband and wife.

Webb's novel offers one of the few antebellum accounts of free black life, and I would submit that his characters and the circumstances in which they find themselves reveal a complexity—indeed, an urgency—about the relationship between freedom and marriage that demands further attention. Participating in, yet removed from, the sentimental conventions of the period, Webb's representation of marriage and the courtship leading up to it is especially charged and complicated. Webb's novel provides perhaps the only account of antebellum African Americans *freely* deciding upon marriage and fully engaged with the pomp and circumstance of the ceremony. Whereas in most sentimental novels the marital contract stands as the apotheosis of the heroine's personal journey, the culmination of her ability to establish loving bonds based on choice, marriage in Webb's novel is a more public affair. Here the heroine's marital decision depends as much upon the nebulous forces of public opinion as it does upon her personal desires. The difference between a free black marriage and a slave-marriage is the fact that the former is not just a private relation: It has public meaning and value.

Without the sanction of public opinion or the protection of law, slave-marriages take on a different character and purpose in these antebellum fictions. Implicitly and explicitly, the novels suggest that slave-marriages—those that fall outside the legal and sentimental conventions of nineteenth-century marriage—are happier, tend to be more fulfilling, and have the potential for equality between the sexes that legal marriages lack. Taken together, these works challenge the supremacy of the law in determining the form and function of marriage in the nineteenth century. By departing in crucial ways from legal conventions of marriage, the slave-marriages these fictions describe illuminate slaves' intimate lives in surprising ways.

If a definitive feature of slavery was the absence of legal marriage, then Reconstruction held out the promise of the law. The slave's freedom became associated with the opportunity to experience the protections and privileges of legal marriage. As Claudia Tate persuasively argues in her reading of "Black Women's Fiction at the Turn-of-the-Century," legal marriage became a sign of both "private prosperity" and "civil justice" for the former slaves and their descendants.[36] The right to marry, as Tate and others have shown, figured

prominently among the bundle of rights former slaves and free blacks valued
in the postbellum years. But marriage was not, as Tate insists, like other political rights. Unlike the right to vote and the right to appropriate the fruits
of one's labor, the right to marry could not be just legislated; it was based as
much on love and mutual attraction as it was on the law. Coming to terms
with the difference between what Tate calls "political desire" and personal
preference is key to understanding the rhetorical and pragmatic aspects of
emancipation as it was implemented after the Civil War.

The activities of the Freedman's Bureau and other such governmental
bodies charged with the task of assisting former slaves make the transition
to freedom relied on legal marriage as "one of the primary instruments by
which citizenship was both developed and managed," but there were several
on both sides of the color line who resisted such efforts.[37] Although slavery
was legally abolished in 1865, slave-marriage extended well after emancipation.
The insistence upon recognizing marriages formed in slavery as a socially and
legally acceptable form of marriage raised a series of perplexing questions
regarding already existing marriage laws and how to integrate former slaves
into American democratic institutions. These questions preoccupy not only
lawmakers and governmental officials but figure prominently in the post-
emancipation fiction. What role would marriage play in the lives of former
slaves? Would the capacity to enter into a legal marriage, as Tate argues, be
sufficient to secure the political and economic rights slaves were denied?

In Frances Harper's novel *Iola Leroy; or, Shadows Uplifted* (1892), the heroine repeatedly rejects a marriage proposal from a man who appears to be a
suitable suitor, because accepting it would deprive her of her black family
and the slave community to which, even after emancipation, she belongs.
Following her period of enslavement, Iola's "search for her true community
and her real family" relies on her marital choice. In the course of her novel,
Harper provides a rationale for limiting marital choice in order to preserve
relations formed by slavery as essential to the social and economic progress
of former slaves.

Focusing on Harper's periodical fiction, written both before and after the
Civil War, chapter 4 examines the tension between slavery and freedom that
distinguishes the form of her fiction. Marital choice is an obsessive theme
of Harper's literary oeuvre. Educating women and men on the criteria of a
suitable partner for marriage remained a constant theme of Harper's pre–
and post–Civil War writings. Harper's antislavery activism went hand in
hand with her critique of marriage, so that—following abolition—Harper's
critique took a not unexpected turn toward racial uplift. In her 1859 short
story, "The Two Offers," Harper presents a radical critique of nineteenth-

century sentimental and legal narratives of marriage, particularly the practice of coverture that made marriage "a mere matter of bargain and sale, or an affair of convenience and selfish interest," rather than "an affinity of souls or a union of hearts." By examining the significance of Harper's principle of marriage as "an affinity of souls" in relation to the abolitionist principles she espoused, I examine her rediscovered stories first published in the *Christian Recorder*. Unlike her later novel, these stories reveal a tension between the material benefits and spiritual costs of marriage, particularly to the public aspirations of her female heroes. Harper's position between women's reform and racial uplift produces stories of unhappy marriages that are literally and figuratively saved by women who find themselves, for various reasons, outside the conventions of marriage. Understanding the broad scope of her fiction allows readers to grasp the precariousness of Harper's political position as a free, black, and *unmarried* woman in the mid-nineteenth century.

Chapter 5, "Wedded to Race: Charles Chesnutt's *Stories of the Color Line,*" focuses on Chesnutt's postslavery fiction and criticism that, in some respects, might be read as offering one of the most effective counterarguments to Harper's view of marriage and vision of freedom. Chesnutt casts a surprisingly critical eye on the movement to legitimate slave-marriages during Reconstruction, a movement celebrated by historians of marriage and slavery alike. Instead, Chesnutt views "the freed people who had sustained to each other the relation of husband and wife as it existed among slaves, [as being] *required by law* to register their consent to continue in the marriage relation. By this simple expedient their former marriages of convenience received the sanction of law"[38] (italics added). Offering slave-marriages "the sanction of law" functioned as a powerful incentive for former slaves to maintain marriages that were formed without consent. Such decisions inscribe an essential difference between black and white forms of marriage since the former signifies a connection to slavery. The differences between their positions are suggestive of a broader political debate about the formation of a postslavery slave community. While Harper views marriage as essential to preserving relations formed in slavery, Chesnutt presents it as a way of breaking free of those relations, of forming new relations that eschew the racial principles that made it impossible for former slaves and their descendants to marry according to self-interest and personal desire.

Each of the authors examined here attempted to show that without public sanction, slave-marriage threatened to destroy the social order of the United States and cause further civil unrest. But in publicizing the perils and pleasures associated with the slave-marriage, these fictions also establish the generic terms of the slave-marriage, thus formulating the terms of a public

sphere that was predicated upon the nonlegal nature of the relation. Affirm-
ing the intimate aspects of slave-marriage through public expression and
suggesting that such publicity might gradually heal the political and social
differences caused by slavery helped to establish a public existence for former
slaves based upon the distinction of their intimate lives. At the same time,
the fictional aspects of the slave-marriage were vital to the coherence and
resilience of what I call a postslavery slave community.

Although my readings of these fictions are grounded in the historical
context in which they were written, they are also guided by a set of aesthetic
and formal questions. What were the rituals of courtship, marriage, and romance for the slave? Given the limited resources and physical constraints of
slavery, how did the slave express affection and sexual desire? What was the
language of love among slaves? Historians of slave culture have attempted to
answer these questions, relying on first-person accounts, testimonials, and
marital records compiled after the Civil War, but these documents reveal
little about the intimate lives of slaves. Although slaves, obviously, could not
marry legally, slave fictions present slaves fully engaged with the rituals of
courtship and marriage that offer a view of the slave experience that cannot
be found elsewhere. While twentieth-century readers of nineteenth-century
slave fiction have complained that such representations are severely limited
by the political discourse of the period, these slave fictions—unlike the slave
narratives—operate within the fictional language of love and desire not only
to depict the ways in which slavery corrupted the slave's sexual experience
but also to show how slavery produced a different set of intimate relations,
creating a language of love and desire that departed in significant ways from
the love stories of most nineteenth-century sentimental fictions. The love
stories of slave fictions are distinguished by the slave's seclusion from civil
society. Without participating in the legal and social conventions governing
proper marital relations, slaves developed relationships that are set outside
the familiar terms of property and contract. The goal of this book, then, is
to begin to map out some of the many ways in which the slave-marriage was
conceived in nineteenth-century fiction, to delineate the relations between
marriage and freedom, and to demonstrate the difference it made for the
fictional slave-marriage to represent not just a romantic and literary ideal
but also a state of affairs that supposedly transcended the law.

1. Between Fiction and Experience

William Wells Brown's *Clotel*

> Marriage—as imposing obligations on the parties to it—has no
> existence here, except in such hearts as are purer and higher than
> the standard morality around them.
>
> Frederick Douglass, *My Bondage and My Freedom*, 1855

One of the earliest historical accounts of slave-marriage appears in *The Narrative of William W. Brown, a Fugitive Slave, Written by Himself* (1847).[1] Marking the beginning of Brown's remarkable literary career that spanned several decades and genres, the *Narrative* introduces readers to a singular personality that was shaped by slavery and a long struggle to acquire freedom. In his introduction, Edmund Quincy highlights the distinction of Brown's *Narrative* by drawing a comparison with the famous *Narrative of the Life of Frederick Douglass* (1845). Brown presents "a different phase of the infernal slave-system from that portrayed in the admirable story by Mr. Douglass."[2] As editor of the *Abolitionist* and *National Anti-Slavery Standard* newspapers, Quincy was an expert on the rhetoric of antislavery arguments.

Central to the differences between Douglass's and Brown's slave narratives (the most popular of their type at the time) were their presentations of marriage. Anna Douglass, Douglass's first wife, plays only a minor role in his life story, though he does offer his marriage certificate at the end of his 1845 *Narrative* as evidence of his freedom. Douglass associates legal marriage with freedom, speaking only of the absence of legal marriage among slaves, and refuses to speak openly of his own intimate experiences in slavery as he writes in his 1855 account of his life: "I need not lift up the veil by giving you any experience of my own."[3] Whatever Douglass's intimate experiences may have been as a slave, they are rendered in his autobiography as only a source of shame. Moreover, Douglass was adamant throughout his life that the story of his own marriage remain an entirely private affair. Though he does admit that there are exceptions to the rule of marriage that he observes in slavery, he provides no single example of such a slave-marriage in any of the three versions of his life story.

Brown's experiences of marriage under slavery are neither as negative nor as simple. Marriage, in Brown's narrative, is noteworthy precisely because it crossed the line between private and public life in surprising ways. The complex ways in which Brown wrote about his experiences of marriage both as a slave and as a free man provide one of the most sustained accounts of slave-marriage in American literature.

◻ ◻ ◻

In his 1853 novel, *Clotel; or, The President's Daughter: A Narrative of Slave Life in the United States*, Brown admonishes "slaveholders [who] do not think [marriage] is of any importance, or of any binding force with their slaves." At the same time, he celebrates slaves who "regard it as a sacred obligation."[4] By doing so, Brown departs in his fiction from the dominant antislavery view that marriage was denied to the slave. Instead, Brown imagines the fact that slaves could not rely on the institutional protection and privileges of legal marriage as producing a different kind of marriage, one that was more lasting and loving than a legal marriage. This view of the slave-marriage now dominates literary and historical accounts of slavery.[5] But it was an idea in Brown's time that was not supported by most autobiographical or factual accounts of slavery. By reading *Clotel* both with and against Brown's empirical accounts of slave-marriage, this chapter examines the ways in which Brown's fictional slave perspective produces a new story of marriage.

Alongside the familiar examples of slave-marriages being broken by traders and owners is the more unusual account of Brown's successful attempt to resist his owner's efforts to arrange his marriage. "[Mrs. Price] would often urge upon me the necessity of having a wife, saying that it would be so pleasant for me to take one in the same family!"[6] The episode is central not only to understanding how Brown finally manages to escape from slavery but also to understanding a vital feature of Brown's character. "People, generally, don't like to tell their love stories to everybody that may think fit to ask about them, and it was so with me."[7] But upon further reflection, Brown realizes that he can use the slave-marriage Mrs. Price arranges against his wishes to his advantage. By making Mrs. Price believe that "Eliza was very dear to [him] indeed, and that nothing but death should part [them]," Brown allays his owner's "fears as to the propriety of taking [him] near a free state." Pretending to be committed—"the same as if [they] were married"—to Eliza, Brown makes the Prices believe that he has no intention of running away.[8] It is, ironically, the slave's performance of marriage that presents Brown with an ideal opportunity to escape. In this way, Brown presents marriage as having the capacity to work both for and against freedom. From the slave owner's perspective, marriage produces affective attachments among slaves that reduce their desire to escape from slavery. But, as Brown's performance reveals, marriage also has the capacity to create opportunities to escape from slavery that might otherwise not exist.

The central role marriage plays in Brown's escape from slavery raises questions as to why these episodes are removed from his later autobiographies, replacing them with more familiar scenes of the slave's acquisition of literacy and wealth. As most of Brown's readers know, Brown constantly revised and borrowed from his earlier publications for various purposes. Indeed, as some critics have argued, Brown's revisions make it almost impossible to discern between the fictional and autobiographical elements of his life story.[9] Written in the third person, the "Narrative of the Life and Escape of William Wells Brown" that serves as the introduction to *Clotel; or, The President's Daughter: A Narrative of Slave Life in the United States* and his later first-person autobiographies, *Memoir of William Wells Brown* (1859) and *My Southern Home; or, The South and Its People* (1880), make no mention of his tumultuous marriage to the free black woman Elizabeth Schooner soon after arriving in Cleveland, Ohio.[10] Brown dwells instead upon his clever efforts to learn to read by bribing two young boys with candy. This episode would be familiar to most readers of the slave narratives. De-emphasizing marriage and playing up literacy makes formal and political sense.[11] The scenes in which he learns to read offer readers a more progressive movement away from slavery and toward freedom, one that ends with the story of his material success rather than the failure of his marriage. Brown's experiences of marriage are more problematic: Not only do his marital experiences set him apart from other slaves, but they also make him appear unconventional, departing from societal norms that discouraged divorce.[12]

Calling this aspect of his autobiographical mode "strategic lying," critics have explained Brown's decision not to include his marital experiences in later versions of his autobiography by citing his interest in presenting himself as "a straightforwardly reliable and trustworthy author."[13] According to this reading, speaking of marriage somehow undermines Brown's authority. Interestingly, Brown removes not only his particular experience of marriage, in which he feigns love for Eliza to dupe Mrs. Price into taking him to a free state, he removes *all* the scenes of marriage that appeared in his 1847 *Narrative* from his later autobiographies. Gone are the stories of the slave Patsey who "was engaged to be married to a man belonging to Major William Christy" and whipped, almost to death, by her master for continuing to see her fiancé after he had forbid her from doing so. Gone too is the story of Sally who was forced to marry Peter soon after her first husband, Ben, was sold, and Lavinia who, like Patsey, was whipped "in such a manner that it was thought she would die" for refusing to marry any other man after "a man to whom she was about to be married was sold."[14] That these scenes of marriage that have little to do with Brown's credibility as a narrator are absent is particularly striking when one realizes that the novel that his later autobiography introduces relies on marriage, as Ann duCille rightly points out, "as a means of exposing the horrors of chattel slavery."[15] Indeed, *Clotel* opens by celebrating marriage, declaring it "the first and most important institution of human existence,"[16] without which society has no moral basis. These deeply troubling episodes of marriage disappear from Brown's life story only to reappear in an entirely new form: slave fiction. Why does Brown need to excise his real-life experiences of marriage in favor of fiction? In the subsequent sections, I examine the ways in which Brown's fiction presents the slave-marriage as an ideal that allows him to leave behind his unhappy encounters with marriage while a slave.

Fiction allows Brown to speak of the slave's marital experiences that the slave narrative's commitment to truth renders virtually impossible. Although Brown speaks of marriage frequently in his *Narrative*, he confesses that his use of the term is misleading, since "there is no such thing as slaves being lawfully married."[17] The "no such thing" of marriage is precisely what distresses Brown. He knows rationally that slave-marriages have no legal effect, and yet he cannot deny, given the overwhelming evidence he witnesses, that marriages between slaves occur and manifest the emotional impact of slavery on citizens and slaves in particularly powerful ways. If there is no such thing as marriage among slaves, what should he call the event or bond that exists between slaves? How to speak of the romantic relationships that exist between slaves and nonslaves? As Brown makes clear in the *Narrative*, he places a great deal of importance on calling things and people by their proper names. In a somewhat narrow sense, Brown's *Narrative* is the story of his name, how he came to be called William Wells Brown. Just as the *Narrative* gives meaning to the name "William Wells Brown," so too does his novel "lift up the veil" that Douglass's *Narrative* creates to cover up the slave's experience of marriage.

Brown's Marital Experience

"In the summer of 1834," Brown explains in his letter addressed to the public, "the same year in which I made my escape from slavery, I unfortunately became acquainted with Miss Betsey Schooner, and after a very short acquaintance, we were married."[18] What follows from this "statement of fact" are the sordid details of Brown's married life that include not only his late realization that his mother-in-law "was living with a second husband, while her first was still alive" and that her "sister was a mother, without having been a wife," but also the more shocking revelation that his wife had committed adultery with his best friend and had had a child with him. Following their separation "by mutual consent" in 1847, Brown decides to reveal the intimate details of his marriage "with great reluctance" on July 12, 1850, in the pages of the antislavery *Liberator* newspaper in response to an article about him entitled "A Stray Husband" that appeared on the front page of the *New York Daily Tribune.*

> Mrs. Elizabeth Brown, wife of William W. Brown, a fugitive slave, (now stumping in England, we believe) sends us a long statement of her conjugal difficulties, the upshot of which is that, notwithstanding she is a very respectable woman and exemplary wife, (which she proves by "no end" of certificates) her husband has deserted her and her youngest child, does nothing for their support, but on the contrary repudiates them both—the former as unfaithful, the latter as spurious.
>
> She says she is penniless and her child destitute, while the husband and father is living in clover, and adds, "Mr. Brown has become so popular among the Abolition ladies that he did not wish his sable wife any longer."[19]

Aside from the impropriety of these public statements concerning Brown's marital life is the fact that his marriage goes against the legal conventions of marriage in nineteenth-century America. Stating that Mrs. Elizabeth Brown is the wife of "a fugitive slave," the *Tribune* publicly recognizes a marriage that could not have been, given the laws of slavery circulating at the time, a legal one. By making the intimate details of Brown's marriage public, both the *Tribune* and the *Liberator* participate in the effort to protect the slave's right to be married. In this respect, Brown presents himself (and slaves generally) as a moral being who has the capacity—despite the failure of the marriage—to live by the laws of marriage even though he is a slave. Interestingly, Brown's marriage is made public only after he and his wife have agreed to separate. As a marriage formed outside the law, Brown's experience of marriage, however unhappy it may have ultimately been, was essential to understanding the definition of marriage he provides in his fiction.

Hidden from law, theirs was a more deeply private, less strategic, more intimate marriage than a legal marriage. However romantic the circumstances of their union, it was also tragic; it is a marriage that ends, notably, with separation and death rather than happily-ever-after, as did more conventional nineteenth-century stories of marriage. Brown suggests that the mistakes he made in his marriage were due to the fact that he was "devotedly attached to her" and that he "loved [his wife] none the less for what [he] had learned in relation to her family."[20] In other words, Brown's love for his wife far outweighed outward appearances, and so he believed that the love he felt for his wife would conquer appearances of her, and her family's, "misconduct."

He was wrong, but Brown's mistake may be due to his ignorance of the conventions of marriage itself; marriage was as much about the joining of two families as it was about the joining of individuals. In her popular history of marriage, Stephanie Coontz dwells at length upon the traditional role marriage played in society: "Because marriage was too important a contract to be left up to the two individuals involved, kin, neighbors, and other outsiders, such as judges, priests, or government officials, were usually involved in negotiating a match."[21] Brown learns the reality of such marriage conventions too late. From the circumstances of his marriage to Elizabeth, Brown's biographer concludes that "[t]heirs must have been a whirlwind, if not cyclonic, courtship."[22] Perhaps, too, Mrs. Price's earlier interventions into his marital life would have made Brown particularly wary of involving others in his decision to marry.

It is only after Elizabeth's improprieties become "widely known" that Brown decides to give up on his marriage. "We then had many conversations respecting a separation." Prior to the publicity of Mrs. Brown's affair, "the helpless condition of [his] children, and [his] infatuated attachment to [his] wife, induced [him] to forego the exposure."[23] In the end, he blames his irrational "attachment" to his wife for acting against his own interests and that of his children. By taking the unusual step of making the private details of his marriage public, Brown goes against, as he himself admits, his personal principles to satisfy the demands of public opinion: "I have been blamed by many for my long silence upon this subject, and even now I give this statement with great reluctance. Nothing but self-defence could possibly have induced me to pen this article."[24] Although he had been "blamed" for his silence, he believes that his silence is justified by his more principled commitment to the idea of marriage itself. Acting against public opinion, Brown believes that marriage should be a private relation, one that should not be discussed with "anyone who should think fit to ask."[25] As a slave, however, Brown must make his marriage public if he wants it to conform to the principles of consent and monogamy regulating the institution.

Brown's experience of marriage exemplifies what Michael Warner points out constitutes the double bind of marriage. Marriage, Warner explains, "is exemplary of the overlapping of private and public contexts since it is thought of in modern culture as the ultimate private relation, but every marriage involves the state if it is to carry the force of law."[26] Married while a fugitive slave, Brown's marriage becomes legal only when he and his wife publicize the details of their married life and separation "by mutual consent."[27] But Brown is not so willing to give up altogether his decidedly modern idea that marriage constitutes an equal relationship between two consenting individuals.

During his life, Brown witnesses several involuntary separations of slave husbands and wives. In the second edition of the *Narrative*, Brown includes his article on "The American Slave-Trade" that originally appeared in the 1848 issue of Maria Weston Chapman's *Liberty Bell*. Excoriating the trade that continues to thrive in the southern states, Brown contends that "[t]his trade presents some of the most revolting and atrocious scenes which can be imagined." Moving away from imagined scenes of slavery to his own experience of slavery, Brown goes on to describe "a scene which took place in the city of St. Louis [between] a man and his wife, both slaves." Although the scene is about the atrocities of the slave trade, particularly its effect on slave-marriages, Brown plays a central role in capturing the feeling of married slaves:

> I watched the countenance of the man while the different persons were bidding on his wife. When his master bid on his wife you could see the smile upon his countenance, and the tears stop; but as soon as another would bid, you could see the countenance change and the tears start afresh. From this change of countenance one could see the workings of the inmost soul. . . . As soon as they became aware that they were to be separated, they both burst into tears; and as she descended from that auction-stand, the husband, walking up to her and taking her by the hand, said, "Well, Fanny, we are to part forever, on earth; you have been a good wife to me, I did all that I could to get my new master to buy you; but he did not want you, and all I have to say is, I hope you will try to meet me in heaven. I shall try to meet you there."[28]

Literature or "literariness" appears in Brown's description of the slave auction he witnesses in at least three distinct ways: in the pervasive irony, in the constant introduction of imaginary examples, and in the frequent use of little fictional dialogues, often presented in indirect discourse—a basic resource of narrative fiction. Brown's method of narrating the breakup of this particular marriage is exemplary of his fictional mode, a "formal strategy," as John Ernest rightly points out, for which "there is no adequate critical term."[29] Brown slips into the fictional mode when he witnesses, as he so often does, the separation of a slave-marriage. Brown's testimony or bearing witness of these events brings the nonlegal marriage into the social world where the idea of marriage has a shared meaning and so has the potential to affect the white audience to whom he addresses this particular scene. He goes on to describe "the countenances of a number of whites who were present, and whose eyes were dim with tears at hearing the man bid his wife farewell."[30] Brown's rhetoric calls to mind a wedding ceremony at which the invited guests are moved to tears by witnessing the couple exchange their matrimonial vows.

Yet Brown makes us understand a slave-marriage in terms of a breakup or separation of a conventional marriage; the slave's experience of involuntary separation distinguished a slave-marriage in at least three distinct ways from a conventional marriage. First, a slave husband and wife could not commit themselves to one another. A slave couple could not establish their own household apart from the slave master. Similarly, a slave husband had little capacity and no legal power to protect his slave wife since her person and her children belonged to the slave master. Since a slave-marriage is commonly characterized in wholly negative terms, it appears odd that slaves would engage in such a relation unless they were forced or coerced to do so by slave owners. But as Brown's examples reveal, this was not the case at all.

Slaves considered their marriages to be, in some respects, above the law; a marriage between slaves has the potential to extend beyond life, as Fanny's slave husband suggests when he tells her that they might be reunited as husband and wife in heaven. Unlike a legal marriage that was predicated upon a property relation between husbands and wives, a slave-marriage was about conjoining souls, a marriage in which the key terms of property and gender simply meant nothing. Set against the contractual terms by which legal marriage is understood, Brown's description of the slave-marriage he witnesses emphasizes the feeling that such a marriage—and separation—produces in both slaves and the free men and women who witness the scene. A slave-marriage is only visible at the moment of separation, at a slave auction, when the couple is sold, separately, to the highest bidder. But as Brown points out, the slave couple's forced separation does little to diminish their desire for attachment to one another. In fact, separation produces the opposite effect. Being forced to separate only strengthens the bond between the slave couple; they are, it appears, more committed to their marriage than those whose marriages are protected by the law.

A Broken Marriage

Clotel introduces readers to a world in which the legal and religious foundations upon which marriage stands have been shattered. Preoccupied by the "degraded and immoral condition" of slavery, *Clotel* opens by citing religious pronouncements on the question of slave-marriage. Quoting directly from the "Shiloh Baptist Association" and the "Savannah River Association," Brown evinces their support of bigamy and adultery to ease the moral panic among slaveholders regarding "the rightfulness of permitting slaves to take to themselves husbands and wives, while they still had others living."[31] Because they put the interests of slaveholders above the principles of marriage, Brown holds these religious teachers directly responsible for destroying what he calls the sanctity of marriage. Condemning the fast and loose approach to marriage encouraged by slaveholders and their sympathizers, Brown's fiction sets out to affirm the importance of upholding the principles of marriage.

Written in opposition to the condition of bigamy and adultery that slaveholders both encourage in their slaves and practice themselves, *Clotel* affirms, we might say, a more proper view of marriage. Whereas slaveholders subscribe to the belief that slaves should "take another husband or wife" in the case of involuntary separation, slaves are unwilling to break the laws against bigamy and adultery. For slaves, marriage "is the most intimate covenant of the heart formed among mankind, and for many persons it is the only relation in which they feel the true sentiments of humanity. It gives scope for every human virtue, since each of these is developed from the love and confidence that here predominate. It unites all that ennobles and beautifies life—sympathy, kindness of will and deed, gratitude, devotion, and every delicate, intimate feeling."[32]

Among its other indications, Brown's notion of the "binding force" of marriage bears the stamp of his unequivocal and sometimes overstated commitment to the law. Whereas slaveholders view marriages among slaves as being essentially different from that of legal marriages, Brown contends here that there should be no variation in the meaning of marriage. Marriage should mean one thing regardless of who or what you are. But the fact is that the meaning of marriage shifts according to contexts. Those religious bodies that were called upon at that time to determine the correct meaning of marriage provided definitions of marriage that served only the interests of slaveholders, going against the principles of marriage. Much of Brown's novel is devoted to correcting the false meanings of marriage disseminated by these "religious teachers"[33] and to provide a consistent and constant meaning of marriage.

Central to the collective experience Brown begins to formulate in 1853 is how slaves "regard [marriage] as a sacred obligation."[34] Here, as elsewhere in Brown's corpus, we are offered an intimate view of slavery by an author who, as he explains in the 1847 *Narrative*, blushes when "the subject of love, courtship, and marriage" is raised.[35] But Brown's blush doesn't exactly express an unwillingness to talk about the subject of marriage, any more than his refusal to marry Eliza expresses his disdain of marriage. His blush indicates his inability to speak of something for which he has no words. If the bond between husband and wife has no legal meaning, what does it mean? Is it, as depicted in the religious documents Brown cites in the opening pages of his fiction, merely a matter of joining two individuals for the sake of physical gratification and, of course, reproduction? Or do slave-marriages provide a different model of marriage from a legal marriage? Might slave-marriages be more lasting, more committed, and more affectionate than a conventional legal marriage? Without an interest in material property, are slaves in a better position to experience the nonmaterial or wholly affective aspects of marriage? As Brown goes on to illustrate through the love triangle that he constructs between Clotel, her lover Horatio Green, and his wife Gertrude, the absence of legal marriage among slaves leads to a more equitable and democratic system of forming intimate relationships, even though it is a relationship that cannot last.

A Bizarre Love Triangle

Horatio and Clotel meet at a "Negro ball," social gatherings that are described as "democratic."[36] The majority of the "attendants" at Brown's Negro balls are "whites" and "quadroon and mulatto girls." While recasting the familiar system of *plaçage*, or what historian Monique Guillory calls "quadroon balls," Brown is more interested in their "democratic" quality—"where gentlemen, shopkeepers, and their clerks, all appear upon terms of perfect equality"— than their essentially unequal racial or sexual character.[37] Brown goes so far as to insist that these balls are far superior to those that take place more exclusively among "white people in the Slave States." At odds with the "quadroon balls" Guillory describes that "flourish in literal and figurative proximity to the slave auction block,"[38] Brown describes the Negro balls as functioning with a "degree of gentility and decorum." By doing so, Brown sets up a rather sharp contrast between the democratic and genteel circumstances that lead to Horatio and Clotel's extralegal union with the unequal and undemocratic circumstances that eventually lead to his legal marriage with Gertrude.

Horatio first meets Gertrude during one of his visits to the house of "a very popular and wealthy man." Induced by his "ambition to become a statesman," Horatio leaves behind "his first love" in order to pursue political success in the arms of a woman who "though inferior in beauty, was yet a pretty contrast to her rival."[39] Significantly, Horatio never loves Gertrude; instead, she "awaken[s] thoughts of the great worldly advantages connected with [such] a union."[40] Like David and Dora in Charles Dickens's well-known novel of the period *David Copperfield* (1850), Horatio and Gertrude are mismatched.

But unlike David Copperfield, Horatio does not suffer from the illusion that he is actually in love with Gertrude. Although their marriage is legal, it is not a loving one nor is it happy. Compared to "the wintry chill" of "polite propriety" that exists between husband and wife, "the gushing love" of the slave is presented as vastly superior to the economic and political benefits of a legal union.[41] However, unlike the unhappy legal union, the more happy, extralegal union is a fragile one, subject not just to forced separation as are most slave-marriages but also to "this new impulse to ambition" and the "strong temptation of variety in love" that characterize free, legal marriages.[42]

Horatio and Gertrude's marriage conforms to the definition of marriage as an economic and political institution with rigid rules. Their marriage is more about property and politics than personal satisfaction. Horatio's relationship with Clotel, and Clotel herself, introduces a less traditional, more equitable form of marriage that departs in crucial ways from its nineteenth-century legal conventions:

> She well knew that a union with her proscribed race was unrecognized by law, and therefore the ceremony would give her no legal hold on Horatio's constancy. But her high poetic nature regarded reality rather than the semblance of things; and when he playfully asked how she could keep him if he wished to run away, she replied, "If the mutual love we have for each other, and the dictates of your own conscience do not cause you to remain my husband, and your affections fall from me, I would not, if I could, hold you by a single fetter."[43]

But, of course, the "marriage" between Horatio and Clotel is mere fiction: It is based upon the lie of Horatio's fidelity. The tension between opposing views of marriage, as at once restricting and enabling personal freedom, are evident here. So too is the tension, one that Brown would continually play with throughout his literary career, between fiction and experience. Echoing, almost verbatim, Lydia Maria Child's short story "The Quadroons," to which he admits to being "indebted" in the novel's conclusion, Brown nonetheless makes certain subtle but significant changes to the story's "quadroon" heroine to suit his divergent political program.[44] Whereas Child's heroine celebrates "the church that my mother loved" to sanction her union, Brown's relies upon the more secular state of "mutual love" and the "dictates of your own conscience." Brown's move away from any association with "the church" is hardly surprising given the critique of "religious teachers" with which he opens the novel and that reaches something of a climax with the introduction of "the Rev. John Peck."[45] Without the recognition of either church or state, Horatio and Clotel's union leaves behind institutions and focuses instead upon the rhetoric of "mutual love" and "affection."

Although the separation of Clotel and Horatio causes considerable anguish on both sides, it departs in crucial ways from the separation of a slave-marriage that Brown witnesses in his own life. Clotel and Horatio separate because he has chosen to marry another woman in order to advance his political career. He had not realized, however, that being legally married would entail having to give up "she [who] would ever be his real wife."[46] Although she is "his slave," she is also "a true woman, and hers was a passion too deep and absorbing to admit of partnership . . . with crime."[47] Echoing, perhaps, Brown's own marital experience, Horatio lacks the understanding to appreciate the true virtues of marriage: "At that moment he would have given worlds to have disengaged himself from Gertrude, but he had gone so far, that blame, disgrace, and duels with angry relatives would now attend any effort to obtain his freedom."[48] Horatio's marriage to Gertrude is determined wholly by the public; he is forced to suppress and later repress his personal feelings, his love for Clotel, in order to participate in politics. Not surprisingly, his feelings for Clotel do not dissipate; to the contrary, they are only intensified by their separation. Separated from Clotel, Horatio's love appears in dreams and revealing facial expressions that ultimately undermine his political ambition. Once Gertrude realizes that he does not love her, she makes up for whatever passion her marriage lacks by destroying Clotel's life and making the child of her husband's first love, Mary, into her slave. In the end, Horatio's decision to forsake his "unfettered" marriage to Clotel for a legal marriage to Gertrude leaves all three worse off. As it turns out, his nonlegal marriage to Clotel provides a far better model of a happy marriage than his legal marriage to Gertrude.

The Rights of Marriage

Alongside the story of Horatio's mistaken ideas about marriage is the more uplifting, but no less tragic, tale of another slave owner's marriage. Georgiana Peck meets her future husband, Carlton, when he visits her father's plantation. Their love is marked not by wealth or even love. Their marriage is marked by a mutual commitment to antislavery principles. "I regret I cannot see eye to eye with you,"[49] Carlton, who embodies the novel's philosophical argument against slavery, says in response to Reverend Peck's long sermon against the existence of "inalienable rights."[50] Representing, one imagines, the author's own views against slavery, Carlton applies the principles of "modern philosophy"[51] to argue that there is "no difference between white men and black men as it regards liberty."[52] Rejecting the Bible outright, Carlton claims to be a "disciple of Rousseau"[53] and looks to "our great Declaration of

Independence" to argue for equal rights.[54] But Carlton's rational argument against slavery is lost on the likes of "the parson poet," whom the narrator presents with disdain and contempt.[55]

If Peck serves as the novel's unequivocal villain, then we might view Carlton, and the philosophy of Rousseau, Voltaire, and Thomas Paine that he espouses, as having the rhetorical power to defeat him. But philosophy and rational thought prove a poor match for Peck's religion of slavery. As a "most cruel master"[56] who interprets the Bible to justify slavery, he "regard[s] all this talk about rights as mere humbug."[57] Since, as he rightly points out, "[t]he Bible is older than the Declaration of Independence" there is no point arguing against him by referring to legal texts and rational thought.[58] The only way to defeat Peck, then, is on his own terms, to argue against him by offering an interpretation of the Bible that abhors, rather than supports, slavery.

Representing the opposite of the religious views her father espouses, Georgiana captures Carlton's heart and eventually joins his abstract ideas of freedom with her more practical interpretation of the Bible. Like Carlton, Georgiana affirms political equality "without regard to colour or condition," but does so as a disciple of "the Lord Jesus Christ" rather than Rousseau.[59] The marital union of this somewhat unlikely pair brings together philosophical and religious ideas about freedom that put into practice Brown's idea of what it means to be free.

Although legal, Georgiana and Carlton's marriage, like a slave-marriage, goes against convention. There are many reasons why the two "should not" marry: "Carlton was poor, and Georgiana was possessed of a large fortune."[60] This fact leads Carlton to avoid proposing marriage, even though he is in love with her. The only way for the couple to overcome the social difference that keeps them apart is to act explicitly against public opinion. It is only after overhearing a conversation between Carlton and the slave Sam, in which Carlton admits to being in love with Georgiana and his belief that his love is not reciprocated, does Georgiana finally get up the nerve to propose marriage. Having read much of "woman's rights" and discussed "the wrongs of woman,"[61] Georgiana is no stranger to the inequalities of marriage. To forge a more equitable relationship, Georgiana proposes to Carlton: "Love and duty triumphed over the woman's timid nature, and that day Georgiana informed Carlton that she was ready to become his wife." Taking the gender reversal a step further, it is, finally, "the young man, with grateful tears [who] accepted."[62] The effects of this felicitous union are almost immediate. "New rules were immediately announced for the working and general treatment of the slaves on the plantation."[63] The unconventional nature of their marriage, a relationship based upon moral principle rather than social status or wealth, leads to an even more radical change in ending the state of inequality inherent to slavery. Georgiana and Carlton's unconventional legal marriage enables Brown, ultimately, to link his argument against slavery with the feminist critique of unequal marriage laws that make women into the property of their husbands.

The law, as women's rights activist Lucy Stone famously argued, made a wife into a "thing," a "nonentity," a "slave." Despite the virtues of legal marriage with which *Clotel* begins, the marriages in the novel present a critique of marriage law that was very much in line with reformers like Stone. In speeches, letters, and pamphlets, reformers declared that women became what the law said they were. If the law said that a wife was a *feme covert*—a being whose identity was covered over, obliterated, who became the property of another, who lost a self—then that is what a wife was. At the same time, female reformers like Stone did not choose to give up on marriage altogether; instead, they imagined themselves as moral beings with the capacity to transform marriage, to make it into a more godly and humane institution.[64] *Clotel* provides these reformers with a model for just such a marriage. Ironically, it is a marriage that is indebted to slavery and Georgiana's efforts to emancipate her slaves upon her father's death. Although Carlton and Georgiana's marriage is equitable, it is not ideal. Georgiana dies too soon, and the couple is thus deprived of the opportunity to live happily ever after. Georgiana and Carlton's marriage is more a matter of political principle than it is of love or mutual desire.

A Necessary Fiction

Clotel concludes with the unlikely marriage of two former slaves: Mary, the daughter of Clotel, and the revolutionary slave George Green, who is sentenced to death after having been convicted of high treason. Echoing the true story of William and Ellen Craft's remarkable escape from slavery, Mary concocts a plan to "exchange clothes" with George in order "to save him from a felon's doom."[65] Although her plan succeeds, George is unable to keep his promise and get Mary out of slavery. The lovers lose sight of each other but are miraculously reunited after a ten-year separation, during which Mary is manumitted through her marriage to a wealthy white man and George, after failing to find Mary, leaves America for England, where he passes for white and puts his slave experiences completely behind him.

When George and Mary meet again in a burial ground in the north of France, they are far removed from the enslaved condition in which they first met. Wandering alone among the green graves and marble tombstones, George pauses to read Roscoe's *Leo X* when Mary appears, dressed in black, and then faints upon recognizing her long-lost lover. These appearances, so carefully chosen by the author, evoke familiar "melancholy" scenes of mysterious women being observed by young gentlemen found in Victorian novels of the period. Participating in the fictional discourse of marriage, Brown presents George and Mary as Victorian subjects with whom his contemporary British audience would have immediately identified. However, he does not let us forget that these Victorian subjects, at least according to American law, are also slaves. "We can but blush for our country's shame," the narrator declares, "when we recall to mind the fact, that while George and Mary Green, and numbers of other fugitives from American slavery, can receive protection from any of the governments of Europe, they cannot return to their native land without becoming slaves."[66] Brown here is referring, no doubt, to his own experience as a fugitive slave. Brown, like George Green, similarly departs for England shortly after he separates from Elizabeth. The passage of the Fugitive Slave Law in 1850 made it impossible for him to return to America without risking being returned to the Prices as their slave. Unlike Brown, however, these slaves "were joined in holy wedlock; so that George and Mary, who had loved each other so ardently in their younger days, were now husband and wife."[67] Although their eventual marriage brings the couple happiness, it does not make them free. Instead, their marriage constitutes "a rare instance of the fidelity of man in the matter of love."[68] At the end of the novel, then, we are offered an image of marital fidelity that is tied—quite specifically—to the slave's experience. Parted from him by slavery, "Mary had every reason to believe that she would never see George again."[69] Like most slaves, Mary probably expected to meet George again only in heaven so, we are told, "we can scarcely find fault with her for marrying Mr. Devenant."[70] But it is George Green's "resolution never to marry, unless to his Mary,"[71] that leaves us with an image of an ideal husband that alludes, once again, to Brown's own experience. Brown revises his unhappy experiences of slave-marriages (both his own and those he witnessed) to produce a happy ending for his fictional slaves. Brown, like George, remains committed to his wife when most men would have long given up on her. Rather than find fault with George's commitment, the novel celebrates his fidelity; such fidelity, which Brown practiced in his own marriage without reward, is recognized and rewarded in his fiction. In Mary and George's relationship, in other words, Brown argues for according the slave-marriage legitimacy through public recognition that fiction alone can offer. Theirs, after all, is a marital fantasy that makes no sense in legal terms. Only through fiction might we understand the love and commitment of a slave-marriage, a rare instance of love that is not bound by law or property.

As a slave novel, *Clotel* offers a paradigmatic example of the cultural work of this form of fiction. Moreover, Brown's novel calls attention to the paradox that slave-marriage represents to our understanding of the intersection between fiction and experience in African American literature. The fact that slave-marriages were not recognized or protected by law made them poignantly fragile; since these unions were subject to the law of slavery rather than the law of marriage, couples were separated and united to further the interests of slaveholders and traders. At the same time, however, it was precisely their position outside the law that made them, for lack of a better term, a model for love marriages. Such marriages were, during Brown's time, replacing the increasingly archaic form of marriage that was grounded in property and politics. *Clotel* helps to provide a language for this new form of marriage, one that had yet to be granted legitimacy. In establishing a new vocabulary for thinking and writing about the slave's experience of love, Brown eschews the autobiographical writing that was so crucial to attaining the antislavery objectives to which he was, for much of his life, bound. Instead, Brown turns to fiction to articulate both his direct and indirect experiences of marriage. Performed without the law, it was only through fiction that the slave's marriage, based on mutual love and affection alone, could be inscribed and realized.

Little is known of Brown's second (but first legal) marriage to Annie Elizabeth Gray in 1860. The only intimate detail of their life together is found in Brown's dedication of the last edition of his novel that appeared in 1867 under the title *Clotelle; or, The Colored Heroine*. There he explains that his wife "so much admired the character of Clotelle as to name [their] daughter after the heroine."[72] Perhaps by naming his daughter after the heroine of his fiction, Brown was finally able to transfer some of the marital happiness found in his novel into his real life. The act of naming his child after his fictional heroine manifests the porous boundary between fiction and history typical of Brown's literary oeuvre. Though the novel offers some clues to the real life of William Wells Brown, his fiction reveals an author struggling to be free of his personal experience.

2. *Dred* and the Freedom of Marriage

Harriet Beecher Stowe's Fiction of Law

Echoing Brown's critique of southern religious teachers who act against the principle of marriage in their support of slavery, Harriet Beecher Stowe draws a similar connection in her 1856 novel, *Dred: A Tale of the Great Dismal Swamp*. Quoting from the "Rev. Robert J. Breckenridge, D.D. a member of the Old School Assembly" in the novel's appendix, ironically entitled "Church Action on Slavery," Stowe reveals the complicity of the Presbyterian Church— "in whose communion the greater part of the slaveholding Presbyterians of the South are found"—of upholding a system that denies legal marriage to all slaves. Breckenridge calls the marriages between slaves "a state of concubinage" rather than marriage because "in the eye of the law, no colored slave-man is the husband of any wife in particular, nor any slave-woman the wife of any husband in particular."[1] From the French adjective *concubinage*, the term refers to the cohabiting of a man and a woman who are not legally married. Although the English translation of the term has a pejorative connotation, in the context of Stowe's second antislavery novel, it signifies an attempt to circumvent the legal terms by which slavery and marriage are defined. By conjoining her argument against slavery with her defense of "the sanctity of marriage," Stowe presents slave-marriage as a relationship that operates according to the principles of higher law.

Slaves, as Brown depicted them in his fictional and autobiographical writings, lacked the legal capacity for matrimony: A slave wife could not commit herself to her slave husband, nor a husband to his wife. She would never live within his household, for a slave could have no household. He had little capacity and no legal power to protect her. Her person and her children belonged to the slave master. Their union was always subject to separation by sale or

gift. According to the legal history, a marriage between slaves could not exist.[2] Marriage, as Alexis de Tocqueville famously observed, was anathema
to the slave because the very condition of the slave made it impossible to
uphold the principles of marriage. "It is easy to perceive," Tocqueville writes,
"that every motive which incites the freedman to a lawful union is lost to the
slave by the simple fact of his slavery."[3] But as this reading of *Dred* begins to
suggest, Stowe did not perceive the matter of marriage among slaves to be
so simple. In fact, Stowe situates marriage at the center of her antislavery
fiction. Slaves might not have had the legal right to marry, but they were married nonetheless. The higher-law tradition Stowe invokes in her rendering
of slave-marriage is complex and includes a wide range of models regarding
the institution of marriage, but her core idea is constant: Marriage must be
a free and equal partnership between a man and a woman based on mutual
affection and desire.

Stowe's definition of marriage departs in crucial ways from the legal terms
of marriage laid out in William Blackstone's *Commentaries on the Laws of England*. "By marriage," Blackstone means "the husband and wife are one person
in law: that is, the very being or legal existence of the woman is suspended
during the marriage or at least is incorporated and consolidated into that of the
husband."[4] Under the legal doctrine of coverture, as described by Blackstone,
the wife's legal identity was effectively absorbed into her husband's. All her
"personal" property was transferred to her husband at the time of the marriage.
The central issue for most mid-nineteenth-century critics of coverture was
that it created and maintained inequality between the sexes. As Sarah Grimké
argued in her account of women's oppression in marriage, "Man seems to feel
that Marriage gives him the control of Woman's person just as the Law gives
him the control of her property. Thus are her most sacred rights destroyed
by that very act, which, under the laws of Nature should enlarge, establish &
protect them."[5] Given the inherently unequal conditions produced by legal
marriage, many argued for abolishing the institution altogether or, at the
very least, loosening its legal constraints by making divorce more accessible.

Stowe opposed any such radical action against marriage. Instead, Stowe
insisted, the problem was not with marriage but in the legal conception of
it. In the plot of her subsequent novel, *The Minister's Wooing* (1859), for instance, Stowe characterizes marriage as "something higher, sweeter, purer,
yet to be attained."[6] Preoccupied primarily with the transfer and ownership
of property, the law only degrades and confines those who choose to become
husband and wife. "Wanting to appropriate a woman as a wife," the novel's
hero, Edward Clayton, insists in the opening pages of *Dred*, "does not, of
course, imply that a man loves her, or that he is capable of loving anything."[7]

Departing from his friends and family on the matter of both marriage and slavery, Clayton represents the novel's unattainable ideal. "Clayton was ideal to an excess; ideality colored every faculty of his mind, and swayed all his reasonings, as an unseen magnet will swerve the needle."[8] While Clayton embodies the right ideals, he does not have the capacity to put his ideas into practice because he is constrained by the limitations of his position as a southern slave-owner and lawyer.

Existing apart from the law, a marriage between slaves provided Stowe with the necessary terms to articulate the condition of an ideal marriage—an ideal, however, that became increasingly difficult to attain when slavery was legally abolished in 1865. In *Dred*, Stowe presents the difference between slave-marriage and legal marriage as a conflict not only between love and the law but also as a broader critique of the novel's conception of intimate relations formed between men and women.[9] Set apart from the legal and generic conventions of marriage, Stowe presents the slave's commitment to and knowledge of marriage as something "higher and purer" than that practiced by free men and women. And in this she not only anticipates recent histories of slave culture that insist that marriages between slaves "served as a means of resistance against oppression" but also begins the complicated process of articulating her own proto-feminist critique of the legal conventions of marriage.

As the women's rights movement took shape in the mid-nineteenth century, it drew upon the legacies of the legal codification movement and the political abolitionist movement to assail the common law, one of the primary sources of women's civil and political status. According to the authors of the six-volume *History of Woman Suffrage*, with the enactment of the married women's property statute in 1848, New York became the first state "to emancipate wives from the slavery of the old common law of England, and to secure to them equal property rights."[10] The parallel between marriage and slavery drawn by several advocates of women's rights was, for Stowe, a troubling one. Like her sister Catherine Beecher and her fellow, but more radical, antislavery novelist Lydia Maria Child, Stowe did not join with the Grimké sisters, Angelina and Sarah, in fusing the political causes of abolition and women's rights before Emancipation.[11] Although Stowe did not join with the mid-nineteenth-century struggle for women's rights, her fiction of this period does reveal that she viewed the status of women and slaves as being intertwined.[12] Advocates of women's rights seized upon the opportunity presented by the married women's property acts to dismantle the rules of the common law that served as the basis for their "slavery," but Stowe viewed the law more critically, or, if we follow her deployment of the law in *Dred*, more creatively.

From start to finish, Stowe's novel is saturated with law and legal texts; as Lisa Whitney notes, "legal matters are so central to *Dred* that it seems to have been written primarily to give them a context."[13] The relationship between law and literature that Stowe develops in her fiction deepens and broadens our understanding of the law. Recent readings of the novel have focused on its liberal use of *State v. Mann,* an 1829 North Carolina Supreme Court opinion written by Justice Thomas Ruffin. Gregg Crane, for instance, examines the ways in which Stowe's antislavery fiction attempts to correct the law, viewing the relationship between the law and literature as generally mutually constitutive. Here I highlight the disjunction between literature and the law at work in Stowe's fiction. Although a number of critics have noted Stowe's complex rhetorical rationale in deploying the case as she does, the bottom line—"The power of the master must be absolute to render the submission of the slave perfect"—relates to the marital relations the novel depicts.[14] Going beyond what was necessary to decide the case, Ruffin analyzes the heart of slavery, declaring that the end of the master–slave relationship is the master's profit, and grounding slavery in power and economics rather than in sentimental or paternalistic notions of mutual benefit and familial affection. Slavery and marriage were both primarily, if not wholly, legal institutions.

But the slave-marriage was not. Set outside legal and economic terms, the slave-marriage, as Stowe shows in her antislavery fiction, operates against the legal and economic terms that determine the condition of both slaves and married women. "People that have friends, and houses, and lands, and money, and all those things, *can't* love as we do," George Harris declares following his miraculous reunion with his slave wife, Eliza, in *Uncle Tom's Cabin.*[15] Prior to their separation, however, George held a very different opinion concerning the state of their union: "Don't you know a slave can't be married? There is no law in this country for that; I can't hold you for my wife, if he chooses to part us."[16] Having separated from his wife in order to avoid a marriage arranged for him by his owner, George realizes that his earlier view of marriage was a mistake. Whereas previously he believed that he could not hold Eliza for his wife if their masters chose to part them, now he knows that slaves like them, "who have nothing but each other," are *more* married than those who are merely legally married. Having been forced to leave his wife once, George Harris would rather die than have to part with her again. Since slave-marriages are predicated on "having nothing," only such marriages are exempt from the legal rhetoric of subjugation and ownership that characterize both slavery and marriage. The subsequent sections of this chapter examine the ways in which the slave's nonlegal experience of marriage enables Stowe to present readers with an example, albeit a fictional one, of an ideal marriage.

Managing Property

Dred begins with a conversation between Harry and Nina Gordon concerning money and marriage. Nina's careless attitude toward both is a matter of some concern for Harry. Paying little attention to Harry's efforts to control her coquettish behavior as well as her spending habits, Nina presents him with a gold watch and a silk dress for his wife, Lisette. Nina's gesture of careless generosity all but demolishes Harry: "A host of conflicting emotions seemed to cross the young man's face, like a shadow of clouds over a field, as he silently undid the packages. His hands trembled, his lips quivered, but he said nothing."[17] The gifts function not only as a kind of peace offering, to make amends for her careless spending, but also suggest the peculiar status of their relationship. We only realize that Harry *belongs* to Nina at the close of the opening chapter.

But Harry is more than that. Not only is Harry Nina's slave, he is also her half-brother and has been charged by their deceased father, Colonel Gordon, with the task of managing "the whole family estate" that has been bequeathed to Nina. "Colonel Gordon thought that, in leaving his plantation under the care of one so energetic, competent, and faithful, as Harry, he had made the best possible provision for his daughter."[18] Property obviously plays an enormous role in determining Harry and Nina's relationship. Harry's deeply emotional reaction to Nina's gifts signifies not only their material value but also their sentimental worth. The gifts are symbols of Harry's semi-free status: He is able to own things, acquire property, and accumulate wealth, even though he is legally a slave. By presenting her slave with such expensive gifts, Nina enables Harry to own property. We learn later that Harry has accumulated almost enough money to purchase his freedom but decides—against his own interests—to give up "five hundred dollars of it" in order to protect his mistress from falling further into debt. Harry's economic relationship with Nina—unspoken and illegitimate though it may be—is key to understanding the fictional world of property, family, and marriage that Stowe's novel inscribes.

According to several historical studies of slavery, the family was important to the formation of the slave community. In these accounts, the slave family provided slaves with the mutual support necessary to withstand the abuses and cruelties of slavery. Although there is considerable evidence to corroborate this conception of the slave family as a self-contained unit existing apart from the slave-owning family, recent studies have begun to suggest that the boundary between owners and slaves was often transgressed. Evidence of such transgressions requires us to rethink definitions of the slave family and plantation household.[19] While *Dred* departs from historical accounts of slavery in several ways, it is also a novel that is interested in documenting history. Rather than providing a dull account of "old empires" and events that occurred "a hundred years ago," Stowe's novel is interested in relating the kind of history that would interest a "young lady who would sit up all night reading a novel."[20] According to its heroine, "a good historical romance is generally truer than a dull history; because it gives some sort of conception of the truth; whereas, the dull history gives none."[21] If we take Nina's literary criticism seriously, as Clayton does, then it makes sense to read *Dred* as a historical fiction of the slave family—a fiction that uncovers the true nature of the intimate relationships formed by slavery.

Introducing readers to three very different nineteenth-century slave-owning families—the Gordons, the Claytons, and the Peytons—Stowe reveals a complex network of relationships that challenge the conventions of American domesticity that she celebrates elsewhere.[22] "Harry was the son of his master, and inherited much of the temper and constitution of his father, tempered by the soft and genial temperament of the beautiful Eboe mulattress who was his mother."[23] The illicit circumstances of Harry's birth are not, as they are in other accounts of sexual relations between slave owners and female slaves of the period, denounced.[24] Instead, "[f]rom this circumstance Harry had received advantages of education very superior to what commonly fell to the lot of his class."[25] Stowe does not mention the nature of the relationship between Harry's parents. We do not know, for instance, if it was consensual. We do know that Colonel Gordon fathered at least two children with his slave since Harry has another sister, Cora, who has married Colonel Gordon's legitimate nephew, George Stewart, with whom she has two illegitimate children of her own. Although Colonel Gordon's legitimate children, Nina and Tom, know nothing of their familial ties to Harry and Cora, they both recognize the singular position Harry occupies on the family estate, which was given the name Canema by "an Indian guide and interpreter, who accompanied the first Col. Gordon as confidential servant."[26]

The history of intimacy between slaves and masters *Dred* depicts goes well beyond the familiar image of Uncle Tom's submission to his various masters. Although Harry is not Nina's legitimate brother, his actions and feelings toward her are more brotherly than that of her legitimate brother, Tom Gordon. Not only does Stowe recognize the bond between master and slave as consanguineous, she also suggests that the novel's illegitimate relationships are more "true" than legitimate or legally sanctioned familial relations.

Harry's method of accumulating property and overseeing the plantation allowed him to proceed, even in the eyes of the legal executors of Colonel Gordon's estate, "with the perfect ease of a free man." Harry's freedom derives not from the color of his skin or even his status as his master's son; instead, it lies in the fact that "everybody, for miles around, knew and respected him."[27] Conforming to a tradition of property ownership and trade that historian Dylan C. Penningroth understands as an extralegal economy that took shape in the South between 1800 and 1880, Harry "proceeded, to all intents and purposes, with the perfect ease of a free man."[28] Arguing that "property ownership and the special efforts it demanded from slaves put an unmistakable dynamism into their social ties, stretching and bending the lines of blood and marriage," Penningroth examines the ways in which slaves developed ties of kinship that were, ultimately, wholly removed from that of slave owners.[29] But as Harry reveals to his slave wife, Lisette, the extralegal status of his property and marriage only deepens and complicates his relationship with Nina, his legal master and illegitimate sister.

Although Harry knows from Colonel Gordon's deathbed confession that he is his oldest son and Nina's half-brother, Nina has no idea of their relation. That Harry chooses to keep their blood ties a secret even though he has ample opportunity to tell her the truth suggests that his love for Nina is predicated on an unspoken attachment, an attachment that has the potential to unhinge the precarious state of their union. Although he loves and admires Nina, he cannot trust her to "do the right thing" with the information their father has so generously and cruelly bestowed upon him. "But, if I should *tell* her; and she shouldn't care, and act as I've seen women act, why then, you know, I couldn't think so any more. I don't *believe* she would, mind you; but, then, I don't like to try."[30] Harry is referring here to mistresses like those depicted by William Wells Brown and Harriet Jacobs who blame their slaves for the sins of their master. Not unlike the affection Uncle Tom expresses for his owner, Harry reveals that it is his emotional and wholly irrational commitment to Nina that prevents him from doing the right thing. In response to Lisette's very logical question—"Why don't you tell her all about it?"—Harry confesses that having "had the care of her all her life" and having promised their father that he would manage the estate until her marriage, he is not going to have his "freedom-papers made out" until she is financially secure and happily married.[31] Harry's commitment to Nina—not unlike his commitment to his slave wife—manifests itself in the form of a promise he made to a dead man and personal history. In other words, Harry has no legal obligation but is motivated by a more familial sense of commitment. And, unlike the commitment between Uncle Tom and his masters, the commitment between Nina and Harry is mutual. Just as Harry's freedom and happiness depend upon Nina's feeling right, so too does Nina rely on Harry's ability to manage her property and make the right marital decision.

Laying out the terms of Nina and Harry's mutually dependent relationship at the outset of the novel is important to understanding Harry's personal investment in Nina's marriage. By beginning the novel in this way, Stowe introduces the threat Nina Gordon, as "a little coquette, flirting, tossing her fan," poses not just to the institution of marriage but also to the situation of her slaves.[32] Marriage is a matter of supreme importance that has the potential not only to change the lives of those entering into it but also of those who happen to be their dependents. As the "Mistress of Canema," Nina holds a considerable fortune; but once she marries, as Harry knows too well, he, along with all the other slaves on the plantation, will become the property of the man she chooses to marry. Therefore, marriage determines the condition of the slave. It is no wonder then that Harry devotes considerable energy to correcting Nina's flawed attitude toward marriage. By recognizing Harry as her true brother and Tom as a false one, Nina gradually progresses toward "feeling right" about both marriage and slavery.

For Harry, marriage is a matter of utmost importance "upon which all happiness depends." Rather than interfere directly with Nina's imprudent decision to be engaged to three gentlemen, Harry asks Nina to judge her actions for herself: "Miss Nina, is that right?" She justifies her actions by raising a few questions of her own: "Why not?—Isn't all fair in war? Don't they trifle with us girls, every chance they get—and sit up so pompous in their rooms, and smoke cigars, and talk us over, as if they only had to put out their finger and say, 'Come here,' to get any of us?"[33] Nina's refusal to submit to the whims of her male suitors, at least to her mind, marks the difference between a woman and a slave. Nina soon learns that her particular brand of battle-of-the-sexes feminism leaves her far worse off. When two of the three gentlemen she is engaged to decide to pay her a visit at the same time, she realizes the foolishness of her former opinion and turns to Harry for advice. And Harry, not surprisingly, is willing to oblige his mistress's request: "Just be perfectly true and open with Mr. Clayton; and, if he and Mr. Carson should come together, just tell him frankly how the matter stands. You are a Gordon, and they say truth always runs in the Gordon blood; and now, Miss Nina, you are no longer a school-girl, but a young lady at the head of the estate."[34] Taking Harry's advice quite seriously, Nina proceeds, with some difficulty, to make Mr. Carson understand that he is "not acceptable" in the most truthful and frank manner possible: "Well, I only want you to think that I am in earnest; and that, though I can *like* you very well as an acquaintance, and shall always wish you well, yet anything else is just as far out of the question as that moon there is from us."[35] Rejecting Mr. Carson's proposal for marriage in this frank and straightforward way reveals that Nina has already begun to shed her coquettish ways so that she can become "the head of the estate." But she cannot do so without Harry's help.

Harry and Nina must join forces in order to protect the family estate from Tom's legitimate claims to the property. Although Tom Gordon is "Colonel Gordon's lawful son," he does not act or feel as a brother should. Instead, he "had contracted a settled ill-will to his sister," and "from childhood, it was his habit to vex and annoy her in every possible way." Compared to her legitimate brother, Nina's illegitimate brother appears to be not only more worthy of the title *brother* but also calls into question the legal and economic terms upon which Tom's legitimacy are based.

Embodying the evils produced by slavery, Tom Gordon does everything he can to destroy the relationship between Nina and Harry. But Nina's commitment to Harry easily withstands Tom's "unprincipled and artful" methods. After surveying the plantation shortly after his arrival, Tom declares that "everything [is] going at sixes and sevens" as a result of "that nigger of a Harry" whom he insists is cheating Nina in order to "feather his own nest."[36] Defending Harry from Tom's groundless accusations, Nina claims, "Harry is an excellent manager. I'm sure nobody could have been more faithful to me; and I am very well satisfied."[37] Her statement does little to satisfy Tom; instead, she only rouses Tom's anger and resentment concerning the terms of their father's will: "All left to you and the executors, as you call them; as if *I* were not the natural guardian of my sister!"[38] By natural, of course, Tom means her legal guardian since he is her lawful brother. Instead, the terms of Colonel Gordon's will make Harry, not Tom, Nina's natural guardian, explicitly going against the legal terms of their familial connection.

Tom's so-called natural connection to his sister amounts to very little since his actions and words reveal that he has not earned the privileges that go along with the title of brother. Nina makes this perfectly clear when he attempts to arrange her marriage for her. "'I shall *not* have him, say what you please; and I *shall* have Mr. Clayton if I choose!' said Nina, with a heightened color. 'You have no right to dictate to me of my own affairs; and I shan't submit to it, I tell you frankly!'"[39] While Nina violently rejects Tom's unwanted marital advice, she turns repeatedly to Harry, not just for help in deciding her "affairs" but also to protect Harry's own marriage from Tom's attempts to interfere with it.

"Harry and His Wife"

Although Harry's marriage does not hold the material consequences or social importance of Nina's, the novel presents his slave-marriage as worth protecting. Indeed, Nina is willing to sell "everything [she's] got—jewels—

everything! . . . before Tom Gordon shall do this thing."[40] The "thing" Tom Gordon plans on doing is to buy Harry's wife, break up their happy marriage, and use Lisette for his own "evil" purposes. Tom's attempts to interfere with Harry's slave-marriage produces in Nina a "sudden burst of passion" that for the first time forces her brother to back down.[41]

Unlike conventional marriages that are based upon "so little of true sincerity, so little real benevolence and charity" or on the acquisition of "a snug little fortune," Harry's marriage to Lisette constitutes "a genuine case of falling in love." The only problem with their marriage is the fact that they are both slaves. Harry "had resolved never to marry, and lay the foundation for a family, until such time as he should be able to have the command of his own destiny, and that of his household. But the charms of a pretty French quadroon overcame the dictates of prudence."[42] Lisette's "charms" conform to the well-known stereotype of the seductive and hypersexualized light-skinned female slave. Departing from the stereotype, however, there is nothing tragic about her. To the contrary, Lisette's optimism remains constant throughout the novel and does much to offset Harry's anxiety.

The relationship between Harry and Lisette personifies the love and happiness promised by a proper marriage. Unlike the majority of Stowe's slave characters who appear either sexless (like Uncle Tom and his wife, Aunt Chloe) or abject victims of their masters' aberrant sexual drives (like Eliza Harris), Harry and Lisette enjoy a healthy and vibrant sexual life. They do not have any children, a notable absence that suggests their sexual energy is not merely for the purposes of reproduction.[43] Instead, this marriage is all about mutual pleasure and enjoyment. Harry and Lisette flirt endlessly, their playful banter punctuated by hands on waists, sitting on knees, and kisses. The couple's happiness is stressed repeatedly and personified by the home they share, which "stood in an enclosure formed by a high hedge of the American holly, whose evergreen foliage and scarlet berries made it, at all times of the year, a beautiful object."[44] Untouched by seasonal changes and removed from other southern cabins, their beautiful home is removed from the world of masters and slaves that surround them.

The physical details Stowe provides about Harry and Lisette's married life bear few signs of the conventions and constraints of a legal marriage. The language of blood, breeding, and fortune is entirely absent in Harry and Lisette's world. We are introduced to the couple, appropriately, on the occasion of Harry's birthday, which Lisette has carefully marked by surprising her husband with a meal that "is good enough for a king!"[45] Their status as slaves does not affect their happiness. "I do think we are the most fortunate people," Lisette declares. "Everything goes just as we want it to."[46] Despite their happiness, Harry knows there is something "wrong" with their marriage. But this knowledge, strangely, does not reduce the couple's pleasure; to the contrary, the precarious state of their union seems only to heighten their pleasure and devotion to one another. Harry tries to explain the problem with their slave-marriage to his carefree wife: "Lisette, I had meant never to have been married till I was a free man; but, somehow, you bewitched me into it."[47] Even though he knows better, his desire to be with Lisette overpowers his sense of reason. In other words, unlike a legal marriage that is entered into rationally, their slave-marriage represents a genuine case of falling head over heels in love. Dismissing Harry's declaration that he was "wrong" to marry *before* securing his freedom, Lisette assures him that "[e]verything will come out right,—you see if it don't, now. I was always lucky, and always shall be."[48] Lisette's optimism is not the consequence of mere superstition, since her marriage to Harry is evidence of her good fortune. Put simply, Lisette believes her marriage will protect her from the evils of slavery.

Lisette's unreserved affection for her husband and his reciprocation of that affection suggests that though their marriage is not legal, it is perfect. She expresses the pleasures of being a slave, not surprisingly, in the form of a song that poorly mimics the vernacular voice of the slave. Lisette sings:

> Me envy not the white man here,
> Though he so proud and gay;
> He great, he proud, he haughty fine,
> While I my banjo play;
> Me work all day, me sleep all night;
> Me have no care, me heart is light;
> Me think not what to-morrow bring;
> Me happy, so me sing.[49]

The sentiments Lisette expresses in her song are plain enough to understand, but the image of the contented slave that her song so obviously evokes is more troubling. Lisette's satisfaction with her enslaved condition makes more sense in a proslavery romance than in Stowe's antislavery romance. How are we to understand the happiness of *Dred*'s slaves? The slave derives her happiness not merely from the generosity of her master but from the fact that she is exempt from the economic pressures and legal constraints that Stowe associates with a proper marriage. Lacking legal recognition, the slave's marriage concerns itself only with the feelings of the couple involved, disregarding the conventional pressures of social or moral obligation. In contrast to Harry's belief that they should have postponed their marriage until after they gained their freedom, Lisette believes that the happiness of their union rests on its absence of legitimacy. But Harry knows better. Without the protection of the law, Harry and Lisette's marriage has the potential to fall apart. The negative and positive differences between a slave's and a master's marriage maintain southern social divisions even after the abolition of slavery.

Harry and Lisette's happiness, predictably, is soon threatened by the return of Nina's legitimate brother who takes over the plantation when Nina dies.

Tom's legitimacy explicitly undermines the marital happiness of the slave couple, but it does not have the power to destroy it. After Nina's death, Harry is no longer bound to the plantation. With Clayton's help, the slave couple overcomes Tom's efforts to break their union and eventually escapes together to the Dismal Swamp, where they continue to enjoy the pleasures of their married life without the material accoutrements. Lisette and Harry have little trouble making a new home for themselves alongside the prophet and rebel Dred in the Great Dismal Swamp. Having lost none of her *joie de vivre*, Lisette continues in her role as a carefree and devoted wife despite the change in their material circumstance. When Harry returns from having a gloomy conversation with Dred about "our afflictions," he finds "Lisette busy within. She ran to meet him, and threw her arms around his neck."[50] The physical gesture suggests that the couple is just as deeply in love as they were before the crisis. Without a pretty cottage and garden, they seem to find as much comfort in one another's arms. Lisette confirms this view as she informs Harry that "I think we could be very happy here. See what a nice bed I have made in this corner, out of leaves and moss! The women are both very kind, and I am glad we have got Old Tiff and the children here. It makes it seem more natural. See, I went out with them, this afternoon, and how many grapes I have got!"[51] Indeed, from Lisette's singular viewpoint, the Dismal Swamp is not dismal at all but rather a kind of Eden before the Fall, in which the lovers make a home from the materials provided by the land and are free from worldly concerns.

The slaves' marriage emblematizes a union that persists despite the absence of legal sanction or economic security. Because their union bypasses the strictures of legal and social convention governing proper marriage, it suggests that the slaves' commitment to marriage might provide those who lack such a commitment with a model for an ideal marriage, one based upon true love and liberty. Slave-marriage in the plot of Stowe's second antislavery novel serves the important function of correcting the terms of a legal marriage, a marriage that Nina Gordon, the novel's antislavery heroine, so vociferously protests.

Protesting Marriage

Prior to becoming the novel's antislavery heroine and martyr, however, Nina Gordon espouses certain feminist principles regarding marriage that at first appear frivolous but, as Harry points out, may cause more harm than she realizes. In response to Clayton's claim that ladies should not read immoral works of literature like Lord Byron's *Don Juan*, Nina describes herself as standing up for her sex by putting down men with her witty retort: "Gentlemen, we ladies are infinitely obliged to you but *we* don't intend to marry people that read naughty books, either. Of course you know snow-flakes don't like smut!"[52] While Harry admits that there is a problem with the double standard regulating the behavior of men and women, he is quick to remind his "mistress" that "some time or other you must marry somebody. You need somebody to take care of the property and place."[53]

Harry's response to Nina's demand for equality between the sexes is, of course, a direct reference to the law of coverture. For all Nina's talk of equal rights, the reality was that the husband had more power than a wife since the husband, as James Kent explains in his popular *Commentaries on American Law (1826–30)*, "becomes entitled, upon the marriage, to all the goods and chattels of the wife, and to the rents and profits of her lands, and he becomes liable to pay her debts and perform her contracts." A legal marriage is as much a business contract as it is a declaration of love and commitment. This is why Harry goes to such lengths to advise his mistress on the subject of marriage. After all, as he explains to Lisette, "On her husband will depend all my happiness for all my life." But as much as Harry is attentive to the law of coverture upon which his happiness so tenuously hangs, so too is he critical of the law that entitles a husband to his wife's property. "O, Lisette!" he complains, "I've seen trouble enough coming of marriages; and I was hoping, you see, that before the time came the money for my freedom would be all paid in, and I should be my own man."[54] Like Nina, Harry worries a great deal about how her inevitable marriage will affect his freedom. Although Harry is a slave and Nina is a slave owner, they are joined by their desire to be free from the law of marriage.

The conjunction between the position of the slave and that of the wife that Stowe draws here is hardly surprising. It is well known that the abolitionist movement gave rise to the women's rights movement by serving as a training ground in political activism.[55] But Stowe was not comfortable with the connection drawn between these two groups. For Stowe, wives were not slaves—although slaves could be wives. Departing from the feminist critique of marriage that equated a married woman with the condition of a slave, Nina's feminism evolves from her early pronouncements against marriage into a kind of holy reverence for the institution and for the man to whom she eventually becomes engaged. The change in Nina's attitude toward marriage parallels her conversion to antislavery principles.

Relying on Harry as she does for marital advice, it is no wonder that Nina never marries. Admonishing herself for being engaged to various men "just for sport," Nina ultimately decides that she "cannot be engaged" to anyone since it produces a most "dreadful feeling."[56] In the end, Nina dies before she can be legally married to Edward Clayton. Nonetheless, they do have the opportunity to be married, like Harry and Lisette, outside the strictures of legal convention. Rather than be engaged, in the conventional sense, the two enjoy an intimacy free of the burdens and responsibilities of a legal marriage. Clayton eases Nina's dread by suggesting an alternative to marriage: "There's no occasion for our being engaged. If you can enjoy being with me and writing to me, why, do it in the freest way, and tomorrow shall take care for the things of itself. . . . There can be no true love without liberty."[57] In the end, Clayton and Nina's ideal marriage resembles a slave-marriage in almost every way, allowing, one imagines, both couples to find freedom through a marriage that exists apart from legal and social convention.

Advising Women

Notwithstanding its explicit antislavery message, Stowe's attention to marriage in *Dred* does not solicit the overwhelming response that made *Uncle Tom's Cabin* such a huge success. Perhaps this is because *Dred* seems curiously preoccupied by marriage, and its argument against slavery is, as Joan Hedrick complains, "encased" in the courtship, engagement, and marriage of its characters.[58] For Hedrick, Stowe's persistent attention to the subject of marriage undoes its antislavery message.[59] Readers expecting the piety of Uncle Tom and the virginal virtue of Little Eva are befuddled by an antislavery heroine who flirts mercilessly and hates to read anything but love letters. While romance may cause *Dred* to be the political and aesthetic failure its critics claim it to be, the romantic elements of Stowe's novel, as this reading of *Dred* has begun to reveal, are essential to understanding its politics.

The novel's departures from its antislavery argument all deal specifically with the question of marriage. While Clayton's unmarried sister, Anne, presents readers with a particularly eloquent critique of marriage, her position against marriage has little practical effect. Embodying the principles of early feminists like Hannah Moore and Mary Wollstonecraft, Anne Clayton's opposition to a marriage between Nina Gordon and her brother is grounded in reason. For Anne, Nina is living proof of the wrongs of women. "I see the plain facts about this young girl; that she is an acknowledged flirt, a noted coquette and jilt; and a woman who is so is necessarily heartless."[60] Dismissing her brother's romantic notions about love and marriage, Anne cites "those good women"—advocates of women's rights—who argue "that a man who chooses his wife as he would a picture in a public exhibition-room, should remember that there is this difference, that the picture cannot go back to the exhibition, but the woman may."[61] Admonishing her brother for choosing to marry a woman who is merely beautiful, she goes on to warn him of the consequences of such a choice. "You have chosen her from seeing her brilliancy in society; but, after all, can you make her happy in the dull routine of a commonplace life?"[62]

For all his sister's sense and sensibility, however, Clayton defeats her arguments against marriage easily. Acknowledging his bride-to-be's shortcomings, Clayton attributes all of them to a single source: poor marital advice. Having grown up "motherless," Nina has been brought up at "a fashionable New York boarding-school," at which she has "developed the talent of shirking lessons, and evading rules, with a taste for side-walk flirtation."[63] What Nina needs is good marital advice, but it is the kind of advice that people like Anne Clayton, who talk of the wrongs and rights of marriage, cannot provide.

That Stowe would turn to the experience of slaves to provide proper marital advice is, of course, ironic. What distinguished the slave's experience of marriage was the fact that a slave could *not* marry. But that fact was only ever a legal fiction used to maintain and protect the absolute power of the master over his slave. In practice, as Stowe's fiction illustrates, slaves were not only married but were married *happily*. So it is no wonder that those slaves who are living happily ever after at the end of this novel provide Nina—and all women—with good marital advice.

Dred concludes with a happy, *legal* marriage between Fanny Peyton and George Russel. But this legal marriage relies in crucial ways upon the advice of a devoted slave whose womanly virtues remind readers of Uncle Tom. But unlike Uncle Tom, Uncle Tiff chooses his own masters. When his mistress, Sue Peyton, dies as the result of a wasteful and negligent husband, Tiff is quick to register his criticism and eventually leaves, taking his dead mistress's children with him. Having become the illegal guardian of Sue's son and daughter, he takes care to ensure that they do not repeat the mistake of their unfortunate mother. Unlike the "soft-hearted" Sue Peyton, who married the degenerate John Cripps when she was too young to know better, Tiff makes sure that her daughter does not repeat her mother's mistake. Following Sue's premature and painful death, Tiff takes it upon himself to protect his mistress's children, Fanny and Teddy, from their immoral father. As a result of the slave's protection, the children are able to reclaim their inheritance and make a new home for themselves in New England, living in "a little Gothic cottage, a perfect gem of rural irregularity and fanciful beauty."[64] This idyllic home is not just cared for by the former slave; it would not exist without his presence. "Yes," said Fanny, "and I sometimes think I don't enjoy it half as well as Uncle Tiff. I'm sure he ought to have some comfort of us, for he worked hard enough for us,—didn't you, Uncle Tiff?"[65] It is no wonder, then, that the man Fanny chooses to marry is one who has been "found" by the slave. Although "[d]is yer an't to be spoke of out loud," Tiff reveals to Clayton that "I's found out he's a right likely man, beside being one of de very fustest old families in de state; and dese yer old families here 'bout as good as dey was in Virginny; and, when all's said and done, it's de men dat's de ting, after all; 'cause a gal can't marry all de generations back, if dey's ever so nice. But he's one of your likeliest men."[66] Like *Dred's* other slaves, Harry and Milly, Tiff exhibits a good deal of knowledge on the subject of marriage. But unlike Harry and Milly's advice to Nina, Tiff's comments are based entirely on his experience of his mistress's marriage. Having devoted himself to protecting "the ancestral greatness of the Peytons" as "he followed his young mistress in her mésalliance with long-suffering devotion," Tiff is in a particularly good position to judge the difference between a good marriage and a bad one. From this slave's perspective, it is of utmost importance to find a man who will be devoted to his wife in sickness and in health, for richer and for poorer—just the kind of man John Cripps was not. In the end, it is the slave who has nothing of his own who knows better than "dese yer women" with property how to choose a good husband.[67]

Tiff, Milly, and Harry all know too well "what comes o' girls marrying high fellows."[68] And so their criteria for a good marriage differ significantly from the proprietary terms of a legal marriage. "Don't care how good-looking dey is, nor what dere manners is,—it's just the ruin of girls that has them."[69] Following a slave's marital advice leads to a much better outcome than following the more conventional advice offered by the spinster Anne Clayton and the widow Mrs. Nesbit. In other words, when Milly tells you, "dis yere one you've got here is a good one, and 'vises you to take him," you had better do so—since, we learn, to do otherwise leads only to a woman's demise.[70]

As it turns out, *Dred's* portrayal of what Stowe called "the legal relations of slavery" is as much about marriage reform as it is about the political crusade to end slavery in the South.[71] At once a critique of the methods of educating and advising women on the subject of marriage, *Dred* presents slave-marriages as examples of nineteenth-century marriages that are more deeply private, less strategic, and more intensely religious than legal marriages. Moreover, Stowe deploys slave-marriages in her novel as definitive of marriage, thereby challenging the legal constitution of marriage and slavery in nineteenth-century America. Given its rather lofty ambitions, it is no wonder that *Dred* failed to achieve its dual political purpose. That is not to say, however, that *Dred* is a failure. To the contrary, without Stowe's legal fiction, readers might never have known the history of a happy slave-marriage and how it helped to free women from the fetters of legal marriage.

3. Free, Black, and Married

Frank J. Webb's *The Garies and Their Friends*

While considering Mr. Walters's marriage proposal, Esther Ellis, the heroine of Frank J. Webb's 1857 novel of black Philadelphia, *The Garies and Their Friends*, sees one "great stumbling block."[1] It is not her lack of affection for her suitor. She loves him. The obstacle is his wealth. Like Nina, Esther turns to her brother for marital advice; but unlike Stowe's white heroine, Esther makes her decisions herself.

Esther decides not to marry the wealthy Mr. Walters because, she says, "everybody would say I married him for that." But so what? "Then *everybody* would lie, *as* everybody very often does!" declares her brother, Charlie Ellis, dismissively.[2] Esther is unconvinced by Charlie's argument and sticks with her decision. When Charlie raises the subject of Esther's marriage again, "Esther blushed and sighed, as she answered: 'No, Charlie, that is all over for the present. I told him yesterday I could not think of marrying now, whilst we are all so unsettled. It grieved me to do it, Charlie, but I felt it was my duty.'"[3]

If this were an ordinary sentimental novel, we would expect Esther to wind up alone and unhappy, realizing her mistake too late. Esther's decision would likely be considered a bad one, exemplifying the consequences of putting "duty" ahead of personal choice. Instead, Esther's refusal indicates the prominent and powerful role that "public opinion," not simply sentiment, plays in Webb's novel.[4] Unlike Esther, the novel's title characters (the Garies) express their "contempt for public opinion" when they decide to marry "in direct opposition to the prejudices of society." Their decision to reject public opinion and follow their hearts results in disaster. They become the first victims of a race riot that leaves the city in ruins.

The Garies and Their Friends ends, like most sentimental novels, with a happy marriage, yet it is decidedly not an ordinary sentimental novel. Although marriages form a significant aspect of the novel's plot, it is Esther's decision *not* to marry the wealthy Walters that reveals how marriage works in the novel. If, as Cindy Weinstein persuasively argues, the purpose of marriage in most sentimental novels signals "an affirmation of the heroine's ability to make a contract,"[5] then Esther's decision to follow "duty" rather than personal desire indicates certain limits to the black heroine's ability to choose whom she will marry. In the two previous chapters, I have been arguing that the slave-marriage offered novelists like Brown and Stowe a way of imagining an ideal marriage: one that was not bound by the fetters of the law but rather by the tendrils of the heart. *The Garies and Their Friends* complicates the differences between the private and public aspects of marriage raised by the slave-marriage. While the slave-marriage may be—as Stowe suggests—a higher or more authentic form of marriage than a legal one, Webb's novel forces us to confront the hard facts of marriage. However much we may want to believe that marriage constitutes a relation between two individuals who choose freely to be together for life, it is a relationship that, for better or for worse, includes an invisible third presence.

The connection between public opinion and marriage with which Webb is preoccupied should come as no surprise since, as Stephanie Coontz argues in her popular account of marriage throughout the ages, only rarely in history "has love been seen as the main reason for getting married."[6] For most of history, marriage was thought to be too vital "an economic and political institution to be left entirely to the free choice of the two individuals involved, especially if they were going to base their decision on something as unreasoning and transitory as love."[7] What is unusual about *The Garies and Their Friends*, however, is that it presents public opinion and love as being two sides of the marriage coin—both are needed for a happy marriage. Whereas Brown's and Stowe's fictions take pains to present the distinction of the slave-marriage from a legal marriage, Webb's novel aims to resolve the tension between the private and public aspects of marriage through its singular antebellum free black marriage plot.

What is a free black marriage, and how does it differ from conventional legal marriage? Although free blacks could, unlike slaves, enter into legal marriages, their racial status seems to have had an impact on marital conventions nonetheless. How did free blacks perceive marriage prior to emancipation? Did marriage curtail or enlarge their free status? While historians have been attentive to the nuances of the "fragile freedom" black Americans enjoyed in the North, the role marriage played in the everyday lives of antebellum free blacks has received only minimal attention.[8] More focused on the cultural, political, and economic conditions of antebellum free blacks, historians have allowed the intimate lives of free blacks to remain largely buried. Through a close analysis of Webb's fiction, this chapter begins to uncover the conventions of free black marriages in antebellum America and the liminal position they occupy between conventional legal marriage and unconventional slave-marriage.

As with Brown, the novelty of Webb's marriage plots may have derived from the circumstances of his own marital experience. Webb wrote and published the novel in London while his wife, the well-known orator Mary Webb, was performing for British audiences. Like the free black characters *The Garies* presents, Frank and Mary Webb were members of Philadelphia's rising black middle class and deployed literature as an instrument of changing the opinions held by those who harbored, as Stowe astutely puts it in the novel's preface, "an intense form of opposition to the free coloured people."[9] Although few historical details about their marriage have been preserved, we do know, from Webb's biographical sketch of his wife, that Mary's performances solicited overwhelming praise from white audiences in the United States and Great Britain.[10] Interestingly, while his wife was something of a literary sensation in her own time—due in no small part to Stowe's personal investment in their literary careers—Webb's novel did not receive the critical attention he had hoped it would attract.[11]

Prompted in part by Claudia Tate and Ann duCille's reassessments of the cultural work of marriage in black women's fiction, *The Garies and Their Friends* is currently experiencing something of literary renaissance.[12] Like the black novels examined by Tate and duCille, marriage and the laws limiting African American access to the institution play a prominent role in Webb's novel. "For a people long-denied the right to marry legally," duCille explains, "marriage is necessarily a historically complex and contradictory concept in African American history and literature."[13] Despite the complications, she continues, legal marriage became the first and most important sign of freedom for black Americans both before and after the Civil War. There is much evidence to substantiate duCille's claims. Perhaps the most convincing source for the connection between legal marriage and freedom in nineteenth-century literature can be found in Frederick Douglass's 1845 autobiography, in which he provides a copy of his own marriage certificate as proof of his freedom.[14] Unlike Douglass's *Narrative* and the post-Reconstruction black novels in which legal marriage functions as a visible sign of the acquisition of individual freedom and citizenship, Webb is preoccupied by the ways in which the legal and social demands of marriage depersonalize the idea of freedom.

The novel opens with Clarence Garie, a slave owner, and Emily Winston, his slave, who live *as if* they are husband and wife on a Georgia plantation. Drawing our attention away from the "peculiar" status of their relationship, we are introduced to their two children, Emily and Clarence, who "showed no trace whatever of African origin."[15] Although the Garies' household appears to be no different from that of other prosperous Southern plantations, we eventually learn that this family only exists in fiction. "To Emily Winston," our narrator explains in a half-apologetic, half-indignant tone, "we have always accorded the title of Mrs. Garie; whilst, in reality, she had no legal claim to it whatever."[16] Making the distinction between reality and fiction explicit, we realize that the Garies' marriage is not real: It is a fiction imagined by the author. And yet the fiction of the Garies' marriage takes on a real or historical dimension when they enter into a legal marriage.

The novel takes us from their luxurious plantation in Georgia to their more functional urban home in Philadelphia, where they transform their fictional marriage into a real one by having a ceremony performed by a minister in the presence of witnesses. Although *The Garies* is neither the first nor the only novel to present readers with a legally married interracial couple, it is perhaps the first novel in which readers witness a legal wedding ceremony between a white master and his female slave. As witnesses, we experience a sense of the dread and foreboding that the event produces. Linking the ceremony with the acts of violence that almost immediately follow the event, Webb situates the Garies' marriage as a discursive site of both coercion and consent. Making their marriage legal does not bring the couple the protection and security they had hoped for. Instead, by marrying against public opinion, their previously safe and content union becomes "fraught with more danger, and open to more annoyances."[17]

In this respect, Webb's novel can be read as an extension of the slave-marriage plot begun by Brown's *Clotel* four years earlier. In *Clotel*, Brown argues against American slave laws that bar Clotel from entering into a legal marriage with her purchaser, Horatio Green. Since Horatio was not legally bound to Clotel, he made the unwise decision of entering into another marriage—legal but loveless—with Gertrude. The tragedy that ensues, Brown insists, could have been avoided if Horatio and Clotel were able to enter into a legal marriage: "The tenderness of Clotel's conscience, together with the care her mother had with her and the high value she placed upon virtue, required an outward marriage; though she well knew that union with her proscribed race was unrecognized by law, and therefore the ceremony would give her no legal hold on Horatio's constancy."[18] In other words, without the law, this marriage is doomed to fail. While Emily and Clarence find themselves in a situation that mirrors that of Clotel and Horatio, there is a crucial difference between the couples: Clarence refuses to keep his love for Emily a secret. Instead, he speaks of it openly and treats their two children with all the care and consideration of a legitimate father.

Unlike Horatio, Clarence has no political ambitions and is willing to make any sacrifice for the sake of making Emily happy. As "a gentleman of superior cultivation," Clarence Garie does not repeat Horatio's fatal mistake. Acting against both self-interest and the advice of friends and relatives to get rid of Emily and the children "in case [he] wanted to marry another woman," Clarence insists upon making a slave into a wife.[19] While Clarence follows a path that veers in the opposite direction of Brown's feckless Horatio, the two meet in tragedy. Although both marriages end in tragedy, Brown's and Webb's fictional accounts of a nonlegal marriage between a mulatta slave and her purchaser were mobilized to very different political ends. *The Garies* contrasts sharply with *Clotel* most obviously because, as several of its critics point out, it does not possess a sustained antislavery argument.[20] It is not with slave law that Webb takes issue; rather, *The Garies and Their Friends* begins to unravel the idea that a legal marriage could also count as a guarantee of civil freedom. The race riot that ends the Garies' legal marriage and separates their children sets into motion the story of a free black marriage, one in which love and the law take a backseat to public opinion.

Down by Law

While Brown and Stowe were decrying the way slavery warped legal and Christian monogamy in their antislavery fictions, Webb's novel depicts a male master and a female slave enjoying a consensual and fruitful intimacy. Moreover, the couple's devotion to one another is all the more intense *because* of Emily Garie's status as a slave. Given the scandalous or inappropriate nature of his relationship with Emily, Clarence has been excluded from most members of his family and his fellow slave owners. That exclusion heightens his commitment to protect Emily and their children from the inequity and prejudice that surrounds them.

Admonishing Emily for referring to their children as "little slaves," Clarence asks, "[H]ow can you speak in that manner? I thought, dear, you regarded me in any other light than that of a master." Emily quickly admits that her husband is "kindness itself" and that she has been blessed in every way with an ideal husband.[21] Although they are happily married, Emily "cannot help feeling" that she is a slave in the eyes of the law "and it makes [her] very sad and unhappy sometimes."[22] What makes Emily so unhappy is not the intimacy she shares with her master. To the contrary, we are told by the novel's entirely reliable narrator, "the connection that might have been productive of many evils, had proved a boon to both."[23] By opening his novel with the rather shocking details of a Georgian slave owner and slave who live as husband and wife, Webb goes on to suggest that their unconventional "marriage" exceeds the qualities of a conventional legal marriage. "I feel that Emily is as much my wife in the eyes of God," Clarence declares, "as if a thousand clergymen had united us. It is not my fault we are not legally married; it is the fault of the laws."[24] Situating their relationship outside the bounds of law and organized religion, Clarence echoes the dictates of higher law that we saw at work in Stowe's antislavery fiction in the previous chapter. Here, however, the higher-law reasoning Clarence exhibits unleashes an anarchic nightmare of subjective (and self-serving) determinations. For all Clarence's good intentions and lofty rhetoric about Emily being his wife, they make little difference to a society dead set against their union.

Given the highly unlikely event of a legal union between a slave and her master in antebellum America, it is hardly surprising that (until recently) *The Garies and Their Friends* was routinely ignored or chastised. In numerous works of antebellum fiction and nonfiction, antislavery authors recount the various ways in which intimate relationships formed between male masters and female slaves went against the consensual and monogamous terms of legal marriage. Predicated upon the inability of the enslaved to exercise her will in any ways other than serving the master, she existed only as an extension or embodiment of the owner's rights of property. Without the legal protections and rights granted by a legal marriage, slave women were vulnerable to what Saidya Hartman calls the "onerous passions" of slave masters.[25] At the same time, the position of the slave as a master's "concubine" ruined or severely compromised the marriage of the free white woman who was forced to endure her husband's infidelity. By depicting the relationship between Clarence and Emily as not just entirely consensual and monogamous but also as a consequence of the otherwise "evil" institution, *The Garies* highlights the possibility that slavery provided a more fertile ground for marriages that were not constrained by racial categories or the law.

While their consensual union may have been "a boon to both," without the law it still bears the stigma of illegitimacy. And it is this stigma that produces so negative a feeling in Emily that Clarence takes the radical step of moving her and their two children to a place where they can enter into a legal marriage. The novel's narrative progression thus traces the Garies' decision to leave the idyllic conditions of their southern home for a more austere life in the North. Ironically, by shifting their marriage from "the eyes of God" to the eyes of the law, the Garies lose the protection of the higher law they had once enjoyed.

Historian Nancy Cott explains that nineteenth-century legal exceptions to intermarriage bans and penalties in mid-Atlantic and New England states did little to undermine the national character of marriage as being between men and women of the same race. Rather, laws criminalizing marriage between whites and persons of color in the South were enforced by mob violence or what Cott calls "extralegal actions" in the North.[26] According to this view, the impetus behind both the New York and Philadelphia mid-nineteenth-century race riots was the event—real or imagined—of an interracial marriage. What the mob was supposedly protesting was not the presence of black Americans but rather the threat their presence posed to the conventions of marriage. Signaling the juxtaposition between marriage and the riot, Webb's novel offers a different understanding of these two public events. While starkly different in form and objective, both southern and northern treatments of such matters rely upon a public expression of a private feeling: Marriage constitutes mutual love, while the mob takes shape around a collective expression of hate. Webb shows that before Emily and Clarence go public with their union they are able to love one another freely, but the moment they enter into a legal relation their love becomes a public affair. The riot is the logical outcome of a marriage that goes against the dictates of public opinion.

In being based on mutual consent and love, the Garies' marriage subscribes to sentimental principles of marriage. But the shift from master and slave to husband and wife that occurs when they seek freedom and legitimacy in Philadelphia does not produce the effect the couple desires. Although there are "no legal difficulties" that prevent them from marrying, the fear of amalgamation that prevailed in Philadelphia and other northern cities at the time casts a shadow on the Garies' desire to marry.[27] Even though there is no law in Philadelphia that prohibits their marriage, the "sentiments respecting coloured people" still stand in their way.[28] "I do not believe in the propriety of amalgamation," the minister Clarence has procured to marry them explains, "and on no consideration could I be induced to assist in the union of a white man or woman with a person who has the slightest infusion of African blood in their veins."[29] Although outraged by the minister's response, Clarence can do little to change his mind. But he does not give up. Instead, with Mr. Ellis's help, he quickly finds another minister who is willing to perform the ceremony "in direct opposition to the prejudices of society."[30] In other words, marriage is constituted not by the law but by the prejudices of society. Marriage, for

Webb, is not just a contract between two individuals; it is in fact a contract between three parties: man, woman, and society.

Whereas Child and Brown imagine that legalizing consensual sexual relations between masters and slaves has the potential to rid the South of the moral corruption caused by slavery, Webb presents Clarence's determination to marry his slave—that is, to give her "a lawful claim to what [she had] already won by faithfulness and devotion"—as a social disturbance, a literal dissolution of the domestic order established by marriage.[31] Although his soon-to-be wife warns him of the possible negative effects of marrying ("it will be a severe trial," she explains to him, "a greater one than you have yet endured for me—and one for which I fear my love will prove but a poor recompense!"), Clarence believes that the law will be enough to protect them from those who are opposed to their union. But this is not the case at all. By gaining legal recognition, the Garies lose the freedom they had once enjoyed as a fictional couple in the South, just as Clarence's Uncle John predicted. "But go to the North," Uncle John ominously warns his nephew, "and it becomes a different thing. Your connection with Emily will inevitably become a matter of notoriety."[32] Though Clarence dismisses his uncle's advice, John's words prove all too true.

Despite having achieved her purpose to become a legal wife, Emily understands the risk she has taken too late. Although she knows that legal recognition of their marriage is crucial to her (and her children's) freedom, she also begins to realize that there is a force higher than the law to which she is equally bound. "It seems," she explains to Clarence, "as if Providence looked unfavourably upon our design; for every time you have attempted it, we have been in some way thwarted."[33] Looked down upon and despised in the South for being "coloured" and for engaging in sexual relations outside of marriage, Emily gains acceptance among the novel's free black characters who "do all in [their] power to aid" the legalization of her marriage.[34] Acting as one of the few witnesses present at their wedding ceremony, Mrs. Ellis reveals that without legal recognition, Emily will remain the subject of gossip and speculation. "Only yesterday," she informs her friend, "that inquisitive Mrs. Tiddy was at our house, and, in conversation respecting you, asked if I knew you to be married to Mr. Garie. I turned the conversation somehow, without giving her a direct answer."[35] Because they are not legally married, Mrs. Ellis cannot speak openly of the Garies' union; she has no choice but to keep her knowledge of the Garies' intimate life to herself. The implication, of course, is that the law authorizes Mrs. Ellis to talk about the Garies. Without the law, Mrs. Ellis must keep what she knows of the Garies' relationship a secret. Once they are legally married, it is implied, Mrs. Ellis and Mrs. Tiddy are able to express their opinions about the couple more freely, and it is ultimately the force of such public opinion that leads to the Garies' demise.

Entering into a legal marriage not only allows Mrs. Ellis to talk freely about the Garies, it also makes them "open to more annoyances," chief of which is their racist next-door neighbor, George Stevens. George is a successful lawyer who "was known in the profession as 'Slippery George,' for the easy manner in which he glided out of scrapes that would have been fatal to the reputation of any other lawyer."[36] George's unethical legal practices are essential to keeping the racial order of Philadelphia in place. Embodying both the force of the law and its malfeasance, George makes it impossible for anyone, other than "the swell gentry of the city," to look to the law for justice.

When Stevens learns of the Garies' marriage, he announces it in order to incite a mob to take action against Clarence Garie: "Oh, he is one of those infernal Abolitionists, and one of the very worst kind; he lives with a nigger woman—and, what is more, he is married to her."[37] The form of Stevens's hate speech is noteworthy. He calls Clarence an Abolitionist, not because he supports the antislavery cause (which as a slave owner he explicitly does not) but because he has performed the single act that most threatens slavery: He has made a slave into a legal wife. Clarence's decision to marry a slave makes him a radical presence that threatens the existing social order upon which George's entire legal practice depends. Echoing Child's argument in support of interracial marriage that "a man has at least as good a right to choose his wife as he has to choose his religion," Clarence naively believes his marriage to be a matter of personal right and preference without considering its social consequences or legal ramifications: "I had the world before me and chose you," he tells Emily on their wedding day, "and with you I am contented to share my lot."[38] Clarence's actions are motivated not by ideology or political commitment; he is, in Child's terms, simply following his heart. But the novel's villain easily exposes Clarence's mistake. Marriage may very well be a relationship dictated by mutual affection and consent, but every marriage exists in "the world" if it is to work. By ignoring what Emily calls the force of "Providence" and what Uncle John calls "notoriety"—or worse, acting against it—Clarence subjects himself, Emily, and their children to its will. Webb thus presents Clarence's decision to make Emily his legal wife as an effort to divorce marriage from its important public function. For this reason, the ensuing violence and death validate the opinions of those characters—Mr. Priestly, Dr. Blackly, and George Stevens—who represent the public opposition to their marriage. Put simply, the law may declare the

Garies married, but without public consent the marriage has either no effect or negative effects.

The Garies' marriage only affirms mistaken sentiments regarding "free coloured people." Their marriage enables Stevens to rally the sentiments of a white mob that, like him, harbors an irrational fear of "amalgamation." After the Garies pay for the legitimacy of marriage with their lives, their children do not reap the rewards of their parents' sacrifice. While the law does not prohibit their union, the law does nothing to protect the sanctity of their union; without such protection, they are left wholly vulnerable to George's racist beliefs and greed. The marriage the Garies had sacrificed so much to secure leads to the dissolution of their family and the destruction of the home belonging to the novel's exemplary free black family. To the public, the Garies' legal marriage signals "the absolute necessity for inflicting some general chastisement, to convince them that they were still negroes, and to teach them to remain in their proper place in the body politic."[39] Once the Garies have been disposed of, the mob moves on to destroy homes belonging to other of the city's free blacks. Free blacks like the Ellises and Walters who own property are, it would seem, as much of a threat to the social order as the Garies' interracial marriage. If the Garies' marriage is the cause of public violence, then peace can only be restored by a proper—that is, a socially acceptable—marriage.

Upon the death of the Garies, Webb turns our attention to their black friends.[40] The only links to the novel's title characters are their "tragic mulatto" children, Clarence and Emily, who are "sold and separated" upon the death of their parents. Emily finds a new home among the Ellises while Clarence is sent away to boarding school in New York, where he embarks upon a life passing as white. The narrative traces their separate paths in the form of yet another marriage plot. Clarence's desire to marry a white woman is thwarted by the intervention of a second George Stevens—the son of the man who murdered his father. Clarence ultimately follows the well-trod path of the tragic mulatto; he dies of a broken heart because the white woman he loves refuses to marry him when his origins are revealed. Following a different path from her interracial family, Emily survives and thrives in the midst of her adopted black family. She secures her connection to the Ellises by marrying Charlie, her adopted brother. Emily's explicit refusal to pass enables her to pursue a life built "upon the blissful state of matrimony."[41] The novel's progression away from the troubled interracial marriage of her parents and toward a marriage that embraces rather than rejects public opinion suggests that the security and prosperity of free blacks relies on a marriage that is as committed to social appearance as it is to personal feeling.

Domestic Violence

Webb's fiction offers a peculiar instance of a legal marriage between a slave and master but does little to resolve the moral problem of sexual relations between masters and slaves. To the contrary, the Garies' relationship manifests all too clearly the sexual aspects of slavery that few, with notable exceptions, were willing to discuss publicly.[42] Although sexual and marital unions between blacks and whites had been a public subject to varying degrees in the antebellum North, the issue had been framed within a critique of slavery and centered on the issue of black women's vulnerability and resistance to rape by white men. Here, however, relations between white men and black women are wholly consensual and, more than that, based upon mutual affection. So absolute is Clarence's faith in the law as an instrument that will protect him and his family that he is willing to give up everything he owns for a legal marriage. As historian Deborah Gray White observes about an earlier period, "Women and blacks were the foundation on which southern white males built their patriarchal regime. If, as seemed to be happening in the North during the 1830s, blacks and women conspired to be other than what white males wanted them to be, the regime would topple."[43] By departing so radically from the conventions of southern white manhood, Clarence Garie poses a serious threat to slavery and the South. The inevitable failure of the novel's legal interracial marriage and the success of its free black marriages suggest that the law does not align with the practice of marriage. For Webb, the law has little effect in determining who marries whom; it is public perception that counts.

Within the imagined universe of the antislavery novel, the problem with slavery lies in its tendency to break up families and threaten the sanctity of marriage. Not only were slave-marriages not recognized by law, but slave masters were also free to have sexual relations with their slaves for the purpose of pleasure or reproduction. Harriet Jacobs's narrative framed her master's frequent and unwanted sexual advances as a matter that destroyed the virtue of black female slaves as well as the lives of many white wives: "The young wife soon learns that the husband in whose hands she has placed her happiness pays no regard to his marriage vows."[44] Such antislavery narratives argued that the only way to abolish the law of slavery was to uphold the law of marriage. So long as slaves could not enter into a legal marriage, all marriages were threatened with dissolution.

Webb's novel presents the fictional or, perhaps more accurately, private marriage between a slave and her owner as ideal. Removed from society, they are able to exist in an "as if" state: one that is not part of the world, a world in which they alone make the rules. But once the Garies leave the South and legalize their union in the free North, they must give up the luxury and comfort of their fictional world and enter the harsh reality of society. In this world, they do not make the rules. Instead, the rules are made and enforced by men of the law like George Stevens. On the surface, the Garies' marriage suggests an amalgamation of blacks and whites that has the potential to upset the social order that George has devoted his legal career to upholding. True to his "Slippery" moniker, however, George finds a way to spin their marriage to his "immense advantage."[45] The Garies' decision to marry allows the corrupt lawyer to enjoy a temporary "triumph" over the law-abiding free blacks.

When the law (in the form of the city's mayor and police) refuses to provide its "coloured citizens" with sufficient protection from the white mob, Walters converts his house "into a temporary fortress."[46] A few of Walters's friends remain behind, including Mr. Ellis, whose own house could not withstand the violence of the mob. He, along with his wife and daughters, Caddy and Esther, find refuge in Walters's house. The presence of women in the house has a transformative effect, and not only in the arrangement of its furniture and the order of the kitchen, as one would expect of women from the domestic discourse of the period. Instead, the women, particularly Esther and Caddy, use their homemaking expertise to help Walters defend his house. The violent ends to which their domestic abilities are put also signify the difference between free black and enslaved womanhood.

In her investigation of African American culture in the free North, Carla Peterson reveals the significant role black women played in public life. By supplementing the existing scholarship on Frederick Douglass, David Walker, Henry Highland Garnet, and Martin Delany with a close look at the work of their female counterparts—Sojourner Truth, Maria Stewart, Jarena Lee, Nancy Prince, Mary Ann Shadd Cary, Frances Ellen Watkins Harper, Sarah Parker Remond, Harriet A. Jacobs, Harriet E. Wilson, and Charlotte Forten— Peterson provides a much-needed vocabulary to discuss the particular experiences of free black women in antebellum America. What we learn from the writings and life experiences of these free black women is how attentive they were to analyzing and responding to the forces of public opinion.[47] These free black women led particularly public lives, and their work manifests a blurring of the boundary between their private and public selves. Often speaking on behalf of those enslaved women who were forced to suffer unwanted sexual advances and pregnancies in silence, these free black women were committed to publicizing the private world of slavery. In these terms, we might consider Webb's heroine, Esther Ellis, to be an exemplary free black woman. But unlike the writers of Peterson's literary-historical study who represent the condition of black Americans in their work, Esther Ellis does more practicing than she does preaching.

While her mother trembles at the sight of guns and other weapons now occupying a prominent position in the home, for Esther their presence produces a change in her "quiet and gentle demeanor,"[48] one that attracts the attention of Walters. Until this moment, the relationship between Walters and Esther had been strictly social. Known throughout the novel as a wealthy black businessman, he appears as a family friend who is more intimate with Esther's father than with Esther herself. His friendship with the Ellis family suggests that they are working toward similar ends and confront similar obstacles. Until the riot, there is no mention of an actual or possible romantic attachment between Esther and Walters, but the riot introduces an intimacy between the two that takes us by surprise.

In an outpouring of anger against whites and sympathy for her fellow blacks, Esther delivers a speech that shocks her family but arouses Walters's attention: "'I say nothing that I do not feel. As we came through the streets to-day, and I saw so many inoffensive creatures, who, like ourselves, have never done these white wretches the least injury,—to see them and us driven from our homes by a mob of wretches, who can accuse us of nothing but being darker than themselves,—it takes all the woman out of my bosom, and make me feel like a—-' here Esther paused, and bit her lip to prevent the utterance of a fierce expression that hovered on the tip of her tongue."[49] Esther is quickly silenced by her mother for departing from the well-known conventions of "true womanhood."[50] "'Hush! Esther, hush! my child; you must not talk so, it sounds unwomanly—unchristian.'"[51] Esther complies with her mother's injunction, but the episode marks her departure from her mother's sentiments: "Esther made no reply, but stood resting her forehead upon the mantelpiece. Her face was flushed with excitement, and her dark eyes glistened like polished jet."[52] The riot arouses in Esther a sexual energy that, while temporarily stifled, seeks release. Her state of "excitement" attracts the attention of the novel's most eligible bachelor: "Mr. Walters stood regarding her for a time with evident admiration, and then said, 'You are a brave one, after my own heart.' Esther hung down her head, confused by the ardent look he cast upon her."[53] Webb deploys the riot as the event that initiates the romance between the novel's chief black characters.

The courtship between Esther and Walters begins while they are engaged in "preparations for defense."[54] Walters discovers Esther alone in the parlor, as the others have taken refuge in the basement. In the dark, Walters enters the room searching for Esther's hand to lead her to the others, as if she were too fearful to move. However, the familiar image of the man leading the woman to safety is disrupted by Esther's insistence that she does not need to be led. Instead, Esther demands that Walters take her pulse as proof of her stable condition: "'Frightened!' she replied; 'I never felt calmer in my life—put your finger on my pulse.'"[55] There is nothing to suggest that the touch is erotically charged. Instead, the contact between Esther and Walters is almost professional; he is touching her wrist and counting the beats to ensure the state of her physical condition, just as a doctor would to assess a patient. As Walters complies with Esther's demand he learns that she is "[s]teady as a clock," substantiating her claim that violence does not intimidate her.

Esther exhibits none of the emotional or physical weakness common to the heroines of white domestic fiction. We might, as have several of Webb's readers, view Esther as exemplifying the virtues of black womanhood.[56] But, as Walters points out, it is Esther's "unwomanly" behavior that makes her the object of his desire: "You have taken me by surprise; but it's always the way with you quiet people; events like these bring you out—seem to change your very natures, as it were."[57] The change Walters observes in Esther's "nature" sparks an extended courtship between the two that ends, many years later, with their marriage.

As in the case of the Garies, violence and love converge in the formation of the union between Esther and Walters. However, unlike Emily Garie, who looks to the law to protect her marriage, Esther's marriage results from having to defend herself from the law: "'Now, Mr. Walters,' said Esther, taking off her bonnet, 'I'm quite in earnest about learning to load these pistols, and I wish you to instruct me.'"[58] A quick study, "Esther gave her undivided attention to the work before her, and when he had finished, she took up another pistol and loaded it with a precision and celerity that would have reflected honour on a more practiced hand."[59] Esther's gun-toting abilities only reinforce Walters's desire: "You'll do, my girl; as I said before, you are one after my own heart."[60] The wealthy Walters weds Esther despite her violations of the accepted norms of female behavior. In doing so, the novel distorts the constraints of marriage that it takes such pains to depict. The marriage between Esther and Walters is a wholly public affair, an affair that makes them literally and figuratively visible. Fully aware of their visibility, they take the necessary precautions to protect both themselves and their family from potential danger.

Homeland Security

Webb's novel represents a world in which public opinion and personal desire converge in marriage. The novel concludes with the wedding of Charlie Ellis and Emily Garie, who "have grown up together,"[61] and the Garie fortune being returned to its rightful heirs following George's gruesome suicide. The wedding between Emily and Charlie is met with much anticipation, as it contains the seeds for black prosperity to grow. The wedding is held in the Walters' home, the same home "from which Walters and his friends made so brave a defence" against George and the white mob.[62] The house bears few signs from "that eventful night . . . save the bullet-hole in the ceiling."[63] The bullet hole serves as a remnant of the past, a particularly violent past that has had a surprisingly positive outcome. Esther, now the head of the household, hosts the wedding at *her* house and is eager to turn it "upside down for [their] mutual benefit."[64] This is a house that has "been turned upside down" on more than one occasion. Turning the house upside down for a wedding rather than a riot reveals a parallel between the two events. Gathered together to discuss "matrimonial arrangements," there is little to remind the happy family of past tragic events. However, Mr. Ellis interrupts their jubilant conversation when the sound of their laughter evokes for him the sound of the mob's attack: "There they come! there they come!" he cries out.[65] Mr. Ellis's cries are a vocal reminder that the circumstances that brought the lovers together—the death of the Garies—shifts the terms of its conventional meaning. Father Banks who, significantly, had been the minister who finally agreed to marry Emily's unfortunate parents, provides the next generation with "some good advice" of his own: "He told them how imperfect and faulty were all mankind—that married life was not all *couleur de rose*—that the trials and cares incident to matrimony fully equaled its pleasures; and besought them to bear with each other patiently, to be charitable to each other's faults—and a reasonable share of earthly happiness must be the result."[66] Marriage, conventionally, is the narrative event that constitutes a happy ending, the event that marks a generic shift from tragedy to comedy. That view of marriage is here tempered—or, literally, blackened—by the destructive effects of the riot. However happy the black couples appear at the novel's conclusion, there is a recognition that their marriages are not like those found in most domestic fictions. These marriages serve as a metaphor for the limits of black freedom or, to put it slightly differently, the end of slavery. Trying to make a home and raise a family amidst an "imperfect and faulty" mankind that feels threatened by the presence of free blacks, they must remain on high alert, prepared at all times to defend themselves against white intrusion. Webb's marriage plot, then, is not merely a romantic affair; it is a matter of conforming to public opinion that determines the domestic condition of blacks in the United States.

Just as in most sentimental fiction of the period, *The Garies* ends with "the blissful state of matrimony" and the promise of future generations enjoying the reward of the domestic stability secured by the marrying couple.[67] Keeping within the conventions of the sentimental novel, Webb's final marriage plot has what Amy Kaplan characterizes as "an incestuous quality [that] unifies the heroine with her adopted 'brother,' usually a childhood playmate or mentor figure."[68] Given the racial dynamics of *The Garies*, the familiar symbolic incest plot takes on a rather different valence from that of many domestic novels set in antebellum America. Whereas most sentimental fiction depicts white characters joined together to keep out racially marked others—Indians, half-breeds, blacks—here marriage occurs between blacks to subdue violent eruptions among whites.

In the case of *The Garies*, Emily renounces her brother by blood in order to marry her adopted brother. Clarence wants his sister to break her engagement to Charlie and join him in New York where he "passes for a white man" and is engaged to marry the white Miss Bates. But his request is met with considerable resistance. Emily writes "a cold" letter in response to Clarence's request; in it she explains that her love for Charlie has replaced any familial affection she had for her brother, implying that she prefers the free black family to the white one her brother has chosen. Emily's decision to marry Charlie turns out to be also a rejection of the interracial and passing marriage plots that ultimately kill both her parents and brother. By choosing to marry Charlie, she is also choosing to comply with public opinion that deems the logic of racial passing an obstacle to the efforts of free blacks to contribute to the prosperity of the society in which they live. The marital union between the Ellises and the Garies with which the novel concludes enacts the desire for a more secure domestic space in which marriage functions as an instrument of mutual benefit and love. Faced with the choice of marrying a black man or passing as white, Emily's decision to marry Charlie rather than return to the home of her "white" brother allows her to live within the bounds of social propriety. If she were to comply with her brother's wishes, she would, as did her parents, fall prey to society's prejudices. And this is exactly what happens to her brother, whose own marriage to the woman he loves is prevented by the young George Stevens. Better to live in society as a free black woman (like her sister-in-law, Esther) than go against the force of public opinion (like her mother, Mrs. Garie).

Webb's fictional account of the historical Philadelphia race riot transforms it into a social event, the site from which the terms of a proper marriage are established. By locating the riot as the beginning of its free black marriage plot, Webb formulates a domestic order that rests upon blacks fully engaged with the economic and social rituals of domestic life. The happy marriages with which Webb's novel concludes symbolize his hope for domestic peace and security following the chaos engendered by the white mob. The chaos that ensues from the Garies' legal marriage is eventually overcome by a series of free black marriages that lead to wealth and prosperity. While it is true that Webb's desire to find a peaceful resolution to the problem of slavery through marriage remains largely outside the political objectives of abolition, the singular free black marriage plot he presents in his novel provides readers with a way of imagining freedom that does not disrupt social order. By witnessing characters whose marriages are based, in Stowe's famous formulation of sentiment, on *feeling right*, Webb's novel presents the difference between a free marriage and a slave-marriage as parallel to the distinction between public and private life; a slave-marriage, then, is one that exists only in fiction while a free marriage must confront, in Frances Harper's apt phrase, the "Trial and Triumph" of real life. More focused on the similarities between free black women and female slaves than is Webb, Harper's fiction of free black womanhood, explored in the following chapter, offers a necessary antidote to Webb's happy ending.

4. "A Legally Unmarried Race"

Frances Harper's Marital Mission

Writing to antebellum African Americans of the free middle class, Frances E. W. Harper's 1859 short story, "The Two Offers," dissolves the distinction between free and slave-marriage so powerfully presented in *The Garies and Their Friends*. Like Frank Webb's underappreciated antebellum novel of free black marriage, Harper's short story introduces readers to a heroine who refuses a conventional marriage in order to fulfill what she perceives to be her social duty. But unlike Webb's Esther Ellis who eventually becomes Mrs. Esther Walters, "No one appended Mrs. to" Harper's Janette Alston.[1]

Published a year prior to the author's own marriage to Fenton Harper—a widower with three children—the story has most often been read as a radical defense of "spinsterhood," echoing the virtues of single life pronounced most famously by the earlier fiction of Catherine Maria Sedgwick.[2] But the story doesn't just end, as does Sedgwick's, with the triumph of the "old maid." Janette Alston instead becomes "an earnest advocate" of "the down-trodden slave" through her writing and eventually gains the happiness and satisfaction that her cousin, the unfortunate Laura Lagrange, fails to achieve through a marriage to a "vain and superficial character."[3]

Celebrating Janette's commitment to literary abolitionism and denouncing the terms of Laura's unhappy marriage, Harper's fiction examines the legal and social conventions of marriage that "looked upon marriage not as a divine sacrament for the soul's development and human progression, but as the title-deed that gave [a husband] possession of the woman he thought he loved."[4] Echoing the well-known analogy between slavery and marriage drawn by prominent women's rights activists of the period, Harper's story alludes here to the condition of women whose property was transferred to their husbands upon marriage. Departing from the dominant nineteenth-century feminist view—espoused most persuasively by Elizabeth Cady Stanton—that women were the hapless victims of marriage laws, Harper holds women who choose to enter into marriage for the sake of material comfort and social appearance responsible for their unhappy condition. Instead, the bond Harper forges in her fiction between free women and slaves emphasizes the rights of slaves, not women.

Although the story originally appeared in the pages of the *Anglo-African Magazine* in 1859, "The Two Offers" seems to have less to do with the "rapidly growing and advanced intelligence of the colored-Race of the present day" than with the condition of the "intellectual woman." The story thus seems somewhat misplaced in a magazine that, in the words of its editor, Thomas Hamilton, was devoted to combating "the endeavor to write down the Negro as something less than a man."[5] Despite the magazine's masculinist rhetoric, Harper's story supplements the essays and stories—of which Martin Delany's serial novel *Blake; or, The Huts of America* was exemplary—describing the strength of black manhood. "The Two Offers" provides a model of womanhood that is directed at her "colored" audience. Rather than aspire simply to marry, women should consider "a higher and better object . . . on the battle-field of existence."[6] In this instance, "the battle-field of existence" refers to political reform. Instead of wedding her life and interests to a spouse, Janette Alston chooses to "willingly espouse an unpopular cause but not an unrighteous one." Unlike a conventional politician who must submit to the will of the people, Janette is in a position to take a more principled political position: one that may not be popular but is right.

Interestingly, Harper's fiction positions marriage, even if it is "a union of hearts," apart from her definition womanhood.[7] Admonishing her literary contemporaries whose poetry and fiction depict a woman "as a frail vine, clinging to her brother man for support, and dying when deprived of it," Harper's fiction counters this image with a woman whose "genius gathered strength from suffering and wondrous power and brilliancy from the agony she hid within the desolate chambers of her soul."[8] Unlike the white heroines of nineteenth-century women's fiction who find happiness and a degree of independence through marriage, Janette's life was like a "beautiful story" and "clothed with the dignity of reality and invested with the sublimity of truth" because she "was an old maid, no husband brightened her life with his love, or shaded it with his neglect."[9] In other words, Harper's story is as much a meditation on the form of fiction—both its pitfalls and possibilities—as it is about the difference between married and single women. Janette does more good and finds greater personal happiness through her "writings" than does Laura by marrying and following the well-known conventions of "true womanhood."[10]

Still, "The Two Offers" is neither anti-marriage nor a defense of marriage. Rather, it epitomizes the seemingly paradoxical connection between the nineteenth-century idealization of marriage and the costs of entering into a marriage that falls short of the ideal. Marriage, the story instructs us, should not be the sole objective for all women. Introducing women to a greater diversity of aspirations, Harper's story offers readers a model of a woman who finds happiness outside the bonds of marriage. We are left to assume that Janette is representative of many women who are ultimately more productive and happy as "old maids" and that there are many, like Laura, who are made worse off by marrying. The story introduces readers to the novel idea, personified by Janette Alston, "that true happiness consists not so much in the fruition of our wishes as in the regulation of desires and the full development and right culture of our whole natures." Read in this way, marriage is only a part of the story; the real story lies in Janette herself, who leads a good and productive life without the support of a husband.

We might also assume that Janette's character would have offered Harper a way of thinking about her own life as a single woman who worked tirelessly defending the rights of the "down-trodden slave" rather than enjoying the freedom that was her birthright. Like Janette, Harper was admired for her eloquence and social commitment; yet at the age of thirty-four when her story first appeared she, too, would have been considered an old maid.[11] Although her story is unmistakably a work of fiction, it—even more than her poems and speeches—reveals a great deal about the author's personal experience as a free black woman engaged in the political battle over slavery. We thus gain insight into Harper's own life and the political position she occupied through her subsequent works of fiction, works in which heroines consistently find happiness by avoiding "the fruition of [their] wishes." Harper's heroines do not merely marry and live happily ever after; instead, they sacrifice their personal happiness in order to do something, as her subsequent and better-known heroine Iola Leroy declares, of "lasting worth for the race."[12] As a result of their sacrifice, they are able to form the kind of marriage that Janette, echoing the feminist credo of the period, describes as "an affinity of souls or a union of hearts."[13] This chapter examines the freedom from the law of marriage Harper forces in her fiction. As a free black feminist-abolitionist, Harper occupies a singular position in the discourse of slave-marriage. In this chapter, I read Harper's fiction in relation to her contemporary women writers who linked the condition of slaves with that of women.

Although several critics have mentioned the significance of Harper's story to both feminist and African American literary histories, it has been largely overlooked by readers of Harper's fiction who remain more focused on her 1892 popular novel, *Iola Leroy; or, Shadows Uplifted*. Generally considered to be "the culmination of her career" that lasted from 1845 to 1900, Harper's novel is central to contemporary considerations of black women's fiction and African American literary history.[14] With the rediscovery of three works of Harper's fiction first published in the *Christian Recorder* between "The Two Offers" and *Iola Leroy*, we now have new insights into Harper's fiction and the theory of marriage embedded within it.

Largely through the efforts of Frances Smith Foster, Harper's periodical fiction has been traced, discovered, and reprinted. These novels—*Minnie's Sacrifice* (1869), *Sowing and Reaping* (1876–1877), *Trial and Triumph* (1888–1889)—constitute a complex critique of the religious and social mores governing marriage during Harper's lifetime. Like *Iola Leroy*, these stories revolve around a female character who decides not to marry for the sake of social appearance or material comfort and is eventually rewarded for choosing more wisely. Unlike her essays and speeches that chastise the current position of women and "coloured people in America," Harper's fiction presents readers with examples of women whose lives embody the virtues she preaches elsewhere. Offering what she calls "ideal beings," her fiction is intended to provide readers with models to imitate. Their appearance in the *Christian Recorder*, the official mouthpiece of the African Methodist Episcopal Church (AME), seems to make better literary-historical sense since the *Recorder* was generally more concerned with women's issues than was the earlier *Anglo-African*. The *Recorder* carried several articles and letters regarding marriage. Each issue prominently announced marriages, identifying the names of the bride and groom as well as the names of the minister and church where the ceremony was performed. The discourse of marriage found in the pages of the *Recorder* was both literary and religious. What is striking about this discourse is the diversity of opinion expressed on the subject. Harper's fiction at once participates in and diverges from the general tenor of this very public and uniquely black conversation on marriage.[15] In this chapter, I focus on Harper's short fiction that appeared in the black periodical press prior to the appearance of her novel. It was through her periodical fiction that she pondered and developed questions of love, marriage, and vocation that are central to *Iola Leroy* and essential to understanding Harper's ideological departures from the metaphoric linking of women and slaves that was ubiquitous during her lifetime.[16]

Writing Her Story

William Still, the well-known black abolitionist and political activist, begins his introduction to *Iola Leroy* with a confession. "I confess," he explains, "when I first learned that Mrs. Harper was about to write 'a story' on some features of the African race, growing out of what was once popularly known as the 'peculiar institution,' I had my doubts about the matter." To be sure, Still's doubts lie only with the form Harper has chosen, not in her "selection of subject." Still does not consider fiction appropriate "for bringing out a work of merit and lasting worth to the race." Against Still's "doubts" and "partial indifference," Harper insists upon fiction to carry out her mission. What Still fails to understand is why a woman "who has come so intimately in contact with the colored people in the South" would choose fiction to document her experience.

Why not tell the story, as Still does in his highly influential work *The Underground Rail Road* (1872), as history?[17] Judging from his account of "Slaves [and] their efforts for Freedom" based upon "Facts, Authentic Narratives, Letters, &c.," Still had little sympathy for or interest in fiction. But he was willing to overlook his prejudice against fiction to "fully indorse her story" because of Harper's other more practical and, to Still's mind, more important work. While still skeptical of the value of fiction to the cause of freedom to which he devoted his life, Still ultimately puts his faith in Harper's good judgment and believes that she would not commit "a blunder which might detract from her own good name." Harper's "good name" was as important to Still as it was to Harper herself, since it was upon her status as "an eminent colored woman" that he concludes his *Underground Railroad*. Writing of Harper's life and work twenty years before the publication of *Iola Leroy*, Still was less doubtful of Harper's critical judgment. "Her mind being of a strictly religious caste, the effusions from her pen all savor of a highly moral and elevating tone."[18] The threat fiction posed to Harper's "good name" raises the question of why Harper chose to depart from her lectures, poetry, and essays—more respectable literary forms in Still's view—to write fiction.

"The Two Offers" and "The Triumph of Freedom—A Dream," both published in the *Anglo-African Magazine*, mark the beginning of Harper's published fiction. While these stories do, as Foster points out, "echo the themes of their author's poetry, letters, and essays," they—like her later periodical fiction—depart in significant ways from Harper's nonfiction and poetry. Harper chose to focus her fiction on women, women who are so virtuous, self-reliant, and brave that they are, as several readers of *Iola Leroy* complain, simply too good to be true.[19] Careful readers find themselves both irritated by her female heroes' virtue and still eager to follow their (impossible) example. For her part, Harper is well aware that her perfect women may strike a false note. But that, as she explains in the conclusion to *Minnie's Sacrifice*, is exactly the point: "And now, in conclusion, may I not ask the indulgence of my readers for a few moments, simply to say that Louis and Minnie are only ideal beings, touched here and there with a coloring from real life?" Despite their fictional status, Harper goes on to "ask that the lesson of Minnie shall have its place among the educational ideas for the advancement of our race?"[20] What is the lesson of Harper's fiction and, more to the point, how will it be used to advance her political cause?

Harper's "colored" female protagonists refuse to accept the fates that the social order decrees for them. Society expects Janette Alston to die of a broken heart, but it is Laura Lagrange, who marries in order to avoid "the risk of being an old maid," who dies sad and alone when she realizes that her husband has forgotten her.[21] Like Janette, Minnie, Belle of *Sowing and Reaping*, Annette of *Trial and Triumph*, and Iola bask in the glory of their self-reliance but, unlike Janette, do eventually marry. Moreover, all of them continue to devote their lives alongside their husbands to lifting up the less fortunate. The marriages Harper depicts in her fiction are, to say the least, unrealistic. Unlike the female protagonists of nineteenth-century women's fiction, Harper's women do not seek or live for marriage alone. Nor do they give up their public lives—as did Harper and, perhaps more famously, Angelina Grimké upon her marriage to Theodore Dwight Weld. Unlike real antislavery women whose marriages eclipse their former political activities, Harper's fictional women experience no such loss. Each of her heroines is lucky enough to marry a man who encourages and assists his wife with her work. When Annette finally marries Luzerne at the end of *Trial and Triumph*, the last of Harper's *Recorder* fictions, their marriage does not interrupt Annette from "doing what she could to teach, help and befriend those on whose chains the rust of ages had gathered."[22] While committed to making Annette his wife, "he [Luzerne] had come not to separate her from her cherished life work, but to help her in uplifting and helping those among whom her lot was cast as a holy benediction, and so after years of trial and pain, their souls had met at last, strengthened by duty, purified by that faith which works by love, and fitted for life's highest truths."[23] In fiction, marriage does not interfere with a woman's career; rather, the two operate in unison, suggesting that marriage does not work unless women do.

Marriage, for Harper, was not the only route for women to obtain happiness or spiritual fulfillment. In fact, marriage could, and did, function as an obstacle to happiness. A loftier purpose defines Harper's women: "She resolved more earnestly than ever to make the world better by her example, gladder by her presence, and to kindle the fires of genius on the altars of universal love and truth."[24] The trick, however, was to convince real women—women who have the flaws of Harper's counterheroines, Laura Lagrange, Jeannette Roland, and Maria Luzerne—to rethink their false notions of marriage as "a mere matter of bargain and sale, or an affair of convenience and selfish interest." Less focused on women's suffrage or the married women's property acts that were at the time central to the women's rights movement, Harper emphasized changing women's minds about what it meant to be real women.

In August 1854 in New Bedford, Massachusetts, Harper began her career as a public lecturer. Writing of her "maiden lecture" officially entitled "The Education and the Elevation of the Colored Race," Harper reveals the event to be "as intellectual a place as any I was ever at of its size." Once launched into the celebrated New England lecture circuit (to be spectacularly denounced by Henry James in his 1886 novel, *The Bostonians*), Harper quickly became a popular and much sought-after speaker. To give readers some sense of Harper's "grueling" schedule, Foster reports that between September 5 and October 20, 1854, she delivered at least thirty-three lectures in twenty-one New England cities and villages.[25] Harper's new work as a lecturer for the Maine Anti-Slavery Society kept her not just busy; it was also a considerable source of pleasure. In a letter to William Still dated September 28, 1854, she writes of "The agent of the State Anti-Slavery Society of Maine [who] travels with me, and she is a pleasant, dear, sweet lady. I do like her so. We travel together, eat together, and sleep together. (She is a white woman.) In fact I have not been in one colored person's house since I left Massachusetts; but I have a pleasant time."[26] Harper's public work seemed to have had a surprisingly favorable effect on her intimate life. While Harper was able to broaden her cultural experiences through her work as a lecturer, she was also acutely aware of her cultural difference, and it was precisely this difference that made some of her accomplishments so remarkable. This connection between her cultural difference and personal accomplishments is even more pronounced in a later letter in which she notes with some pride that "a short while ago when I was down this way I took breakfast with the then Governor of Maine."[27] Although Harper's public career has been well documented, little has been written about its impact on her private life and her conception of the domestic world that was the purview of most women. Breakfasting with the governor of Maine gave her a sense of the importance of her mission and her political influence. While Harper's experiences of traveling on the road as an antislavery lecturer certainly are not far from the experiences of a typical politician or public official, it would be a mistake to view her as such. As a black woman, her voice did not carry the clout or significance of her male counterparts. But, as her personal correspondence and reviews of her lectures reveal, Harper was nonetheless an influential public figure and privately reveled in the glow of her celebrity status.

Harper's public career was interrupted, briefly, by her marriage to Fenton Harper on November 22, 1860. No longer available to travel, Harper settled down to perform the duties of a housewife and mother of four. Although Harper remained committed to the antislavery cause, she did so from home. In his brief biography, Still explains that "Notwithstanding her family cares, consequent upon married life, she only ceased from her literary and Anti-slavery labors, when compelled to do so by other duties."[28] During the four years of her marriage, Harper confined herself to speaking to smaller audiences located close to her home near Columbus, Ohio. However, within just five months of her husband's death, "the papers were once again advertising her public lectures" in New England.[29] Marriage, at least in Harper's experience of it, was not compatible with having a public life. There are few details that might clarify the terms of Harper's marriage. How did she meet Fenton? Were they in love? Was her decision to marry the widower a sacrifice? Or did she derive some pleasure from no longer being an "old maid"? Did Harper believe, like Laura Lagrange, that any offer of marriage was better than no offer? It is impossible to answer these questions because Harper never once mentions her marriage, or the circumstances leading up to it, in any of her writings.

We do know, however, that she used her own earnings to pay for the farm-house in which the couple lived. Harper makes only a single reference to her marriage, in a rather fiery speech delivered at the eleventh National Women's Rights Convention in May 1866. Given the forum in which she spoke, it is no wonder that she reveals little of their intimate life. Indeed, she does not even refer to her husband by his proper name. Judging from what she does reveal about her marriage, it did not end well for her:

> But my husband died in debt; and before he had been in his grave three months, the administrator had swept the very milk-crocks and wash tubs from my hands. I was a farmer's wife and made butter for the Columbus market; but what could I do, when they swept all away? They left me one thing—and that was a looking-glass! Had I died instead of my husband, how different would have been the result! By this time he would have had another wife, it is likely; and no administrator would have gone into his house, broken up his home, and sold his bed, and taken away his means of support. . . . I say, then, that justice is not fulfilled so long as woman is unequal before the law.[30]

While Harper begins her speech by expressing solidarity with those women who had organized the convention—Stanton and Susan B. Anthony, along-side the National Woman Suffrage Association, were its primary architects—

she concludes by setting herself in opposition to their goals, going so far as to suggest that they rethink their political commitments altogether. Speaking directly to the prominent white women gathered at the convention, Harper declares, "I tell you that if there is any class of people who need to be lifted out of their airy nothings and selfishness, it is the white women of America." Marking herself as black and speaking on behalf of black women, Harper here notes the material differences between black and white women that the latter, we assume, are entirely ignorant of.[31] Unlike white women who derived their status from that of their husbands, black women could not rely on their husbands. Moreover, black women had no legal means of protecting their property upon the death of their husbands. Admonishing white women for speaking of their rights without considering the privilege of their situation, Harper sets herself apart from the women's rights movement. "You white women speak here of rights. I speak of wrongs. I, as a colored woman, have had in this country an education which has made me feel as if I were in the situation of Ishmael, my hand against every man, and every man's hand against me."[32]

What are we to make of the audaciousness of Harper's declaration? Her critique of the organizers of the convention by whom she was invited to speak seems on the one hand inappropriate and on the other entirely appropriate. Obviously, her critique would be far more effective if she could ensure that those she was criticizing were listening. But she would also be setting herself apart from white women, marking her difference in a way that goes against her personal experience of traveling with white women during her time as a lecturer for the Maine Anti-Slavery Society. Her speech also gives her the opportunity to speak publicly about the consequences of her marriage on her personal circumstances. Interestingly, Harper reveals these details not to solicit sympathy but to mark the difference between her life and that of her listeners. But it is not against actual white women that Harper speaks. It is "their airy nothings and selfishness" manifested most visibly in their notions of marriage. Deploying her own marriage as example, Harper argues that marriage is hard work, a form of labor that brings little pleasure but is necessary nonetheless. Harper diverged from the women's movement in her conception of marriage as a form of sacrificial labor that is performed for the good of others and society as a whole.

From this view, Harper's theory of marriage seems no different from that which circulated weekly in the pages of the *Christian Recorder*. Seeking in part to replace popular stereotypes of Africans as primitive, irresponsible, and lustful with proof of their civilized, disciplined, and moral behavior, the *Recorder* carried several letters and essays advocating the rightness of monogamous marriage. On February 9, 1861, for instance, the *Recorder* published a letter from W. D. W. Schureman that began "Mr. Editor:—I propose writing a few practical thoughts on [marriage]. . . . Marriage is the union of sexes, under matrimonial obligations. It is the proper mode to carry out a Divine mandate." The basic assumption in Schureman's letter is that marriage should be a lifelong commitment. It follows that he would declare "a misstep in marriage" to be "one of the greatest curses known to domestic life, or the public community." His letter constitutes an effort to help readers avoid such tragedies by reminding them of the real purpose of marriage. "How few understand the great and important object of matrimony," he wrote. "Some think it is to unite with a pretty or handsome person, or to satisfy amative desire; to accumulate riches, to show our independence, and thereby spite others; to have a home, to have a cover, to appear like others."

Schureman does not clarify where these false notions of marriage come from. It could be that such notions derived from slavery where, as William Wells Brown reveals in both his novel and autobiography, slaveholders viewed marriage without having "any binding force with their slaves."[33] Schureman's insistence on "the honesty and truthfulness" of his "few practical thoughts on marriage" might also point to fiction as the cause of the "missteps in marriage" he so emphatically denounces. It was, after all, sentimental fiction of the period—popular novels by Susan Warner, Mary Hayden Green Pike, and E. D. E. N. Southworth—that explicitly went against Schureman's principles. In their sentimental novels, marriage was represented as a means "to satisfy amative desire; to accumulate riches, to show our independence, and thereby spite others; to have a home, to have a cover, to appear like others." For Schureman and other writers and readers of the *Recorder*, defining marriage against such "airy nothings" was a matter of supreme importance. "The object of matrimony," he informs us, "is to glorify God; under its varied facilities to serve him with our body and sprit, which are his. Thus preparing ourselves for usefulness here and heaven hereafter; to train up our children in the way they should go, that when they become old they may not depart from it."

Part of the urgency of this objective lay in the widespread assumption that the majority of black Americans, having been slaves, had, in Harper's words, "to be taught the sacredness of the marriage relation."[34] But unlike Schureman and others who expostulated on the sacredness of marriage, Harper was primarily interested in how women, particularly black women like herself, figured in the marriage relation. The difference between black and white women often ascribed to race, as Cindy Weinstein points out, turns instead on the question of marriage. "Sentimental fictions' insistence on the marriage contract as the embodiment of an ideal of family based on choice ... takes on different meanings when understood in relation to the fact that slave law mandated marriage as a contract into which slaves could not enter."[35] While this fact has most often been interpreted as producing, in Claudia Tate's terms, a "political desire" on the part of black women for marriage, it also had the effect of producing a desire to merge, or even eclipse, the private world of matrimony and motherhood with a public life. In other words, Harper's particular brand of feminism constitutes a critique of women who believed marriage could fulfill their desires. For Harper, satisfaction was derived from her work—writing and lecturing—not marriage.

A Higher, Holier Destiny

On March 13, 1869, the *Christian Recorder* introduced *Minnie's Sacrifice* as "the title of a serial story to be contributed by Mrs. F. E. W. Harper." The publication of the story seems to have been something of a coup for the *Recorder* since the editors go on to "congratulate [their] readers on making this announcement." After all, "[a]s a writer, whether of prose or poetry, Mrs. Harper stands foremost of all the colored women of our day; while, as a speaker, she has been by many favorably compared to Annie Dickinson." As well-known antislavery and women's rights lecturers, comparisons between Harper and Dickinson were frequent and not at all surprising. Dickinson had just published her first novel, *What Answer?* (1868), of a doomed interracial marriage to considerable critical acclaim.[36] The novel first appeared in the fall of 1868, less than a year before the *Recorder* announced the publication of *Minnie's Sacrifice*. Although there is no evidence to suggest that Harper and Dickinson were personally acquainted, their common interests and talents would have surely brought the two together. Indeed, the frequent comparisons between the two women might help us to understand Harper's fictional heroine Minnie who, like Dickinson's Francesca Ercildoune, is of mixed racial parentage. But unlike Francesca, Minnie does not knowingly pass as white. In the concluding chapter of *Minnie's Sacrifice*, Harper makes the difference between her marriage plot and that of other contemporary fictions the point of the story: "While some of the authors of the present day have been weaving their stories about white men marrying beautiful quadroon girls, who, in so doing were lost to us socially, I conceived of one of that same class to whom I gave a higher, holier destiny; a life of lofty self-sacrifice and beautiful self-consecration, finished at the post of duty, and rounded off with the fiery crown of martyrdom, a circlet which ever changes into a diadem of glory."[37] Although Harper does not refer to Dickinson's novel by name, her concluding remarks help to contextualize a story that might otherwise be bound to the religious rhetoric of marriage espoused by the *Recorder*'s less noteworthy contributors.[38]

Dickinson's novel centers on a romance between Willie Surrey, a wealthy young New Yorker, and Francesca Ercildoune. Willie falls in love with Francesca, not realizing that her father is black; she is able to pass for white. Many misunderstandings between the couple ensue, in which Francesca rejects Willie because she wrongly presumes that he shares the racist views espoused by his parents. But the war between North and South leads Francesca to realize her mistake. Willie joins the Union Army, loses an arm in battle, and returns to woo, win, and wed Francesca, planning afterward to recruit and lead a black brigade, perhaps as added proof of his commitment to the race with which his bride is aligned.[39] Their marriage, performed over the objections of the Surrey family and the disapproval of most of Willie's friends, constitutes the novel's high point. It is to be read as a rare instance of love conquering racial prejudice. And it is rendered all the more poignant when Francesca and Willie die in one another's arms as a result of an angry white mob protesting the draft in the city of New York.[40] "There it stirred; the eyes unclosed to meet hers, a gleam of divine love shining through their fading fire; the battered, stiffened arm lifted, as to fold her in the old familiar caress. 'Darling—die—to make—free'—came in gasps from the sweet, yet whitening lips. Then she lay still."[41] *What Answer?* can also be read as an extension of Dickinson's postwar reform work that was directed almost entirely in support of black suffrage. The last page of her novel describes a maimed black veteran's ill-fated attempt to vote, and she ends the novel, not unlike Harper's own concluding remarks, by expressing the political purposes lying behind her fiction. "I have written this book," she informs us in her note that provides readers with a list of her nonfictional sources, "and send it to the consciences and the hearts of the American people. May God, for whose 'little ones' I have here spoken, vivify its words."[42]

Though Francesca is beautiful and virtuous, like the majority of Harper's fictional heroines, who marries for love rather than convenience or self-interest, she, like her white husband and black father, embodies the life of the idle rich. Francesca doesn't do anything in this novel but get married and die. Although their marriage removes them from the prejudices of their society, it does little to protect them from reality. "An idle, happy time! A time to make a worker sigh only to behold, and a Benthamite lift his hands in depreciation and despair. A time which would not last, because it could not, any more than apple-blossoms and May flowers, but which was sweet and fragrant past all describing while it endured."[43] Although Dickinson acknowledges that such a marriage is pure fiction, a temporary state of bliss that could not last, she does nonetheless celebrate the love of this marriage, a love that is willing to sacrifice social censure and even death. But in the end, the passing and interracial marriage plots of Dickinson's novel don't do much for the novel's black characters. The story concludes with the marriage of a white working-class couple who has been figuratively adopted by Francesca's black father. They enjoy the material benefits that would have gone to Francesca if she and her husband had not died.

That Dickinson chooses to depict such a scenario as the answer to the racial violence and inequity of post–Civil War America would likely have infuriated Harper—as it did other prominent women's rights proponents such as Stanton, who felt that Dickinson's novel had betrayed women for the sake of black suffrage.[44] Evidence of Harper's contempt for the "airy nothings and selfishness" of "the white women of America" can be found in the character of Camilla La Croix, who sets the plot of *Minnie's Sacrifice* into motion. Although there is nothing evil about Camilla—she seems to be well intentioned and generous for the daughter of a slave owner who rapes his female slaves and feels little remorse—she is naïve and spoiled. In her efforts to save Miriam's grandson from "being a slave," Camilla proposes "to ask Pa, to let [her] take him to the house, and have a nurse for him, and bring him up like a white child, and never let him know that he is colored." And because her father never refuses his daughter anything she sets her heart upon, even a two-thousand-dollar necklace from Tiffany's, she is certain her father will consent to her plan.[45] Camilla's lackadaisical attitude toward slavery changes, however, when she witnesses a former slave give a lecture "about the wrongs which had been heaped upon him" while he was a slave in the South.[46] For the first time in her life, Camilla moves beyond having sympathy for her slaves and takes action against slavery: "What she had seen of slavery in the South had awakened her sympathy and compassion. What she had heard of it in the North had aroused her sense of justice. She had seen the old system under a new light. The good seed was planted, which was yet to yield its harvest of blessed deeds."[47] Camilla's conversion to antislavery politics produces immediate results. No longer the spoiled daughter of a slave owner, Camilla marries "a gentleman from the North" and tries "to do all in her power to ameliorate the condition of her slaves; still she is not satisfied with the system, and is trying to prepare her slaves for freedom."[48] But Camilla's conversion is not complete. Her decision to keep her "adopted brother's" identity a secret in order to protect him from the truth produces bad results. Unconscious of the truth, Louis, her half-brother, becomes an ardent defender of slavery and the South. However well intentioned Camilla may be, Camilla falls short of meeting Harper's ideal. Camilla is rich and happy, a condition that prevents her from understanding how it feels to be a slave or what it means to be black. Depriving her brother of that experience, as Louis declares, is a mistake. "I think," said Louis facing the floor, "that a cruel wrong was done to Minnie and myself when life was given to us under conditions that doomed us to hopeless slavery, and from which we were rescued only by good fortune. I have heard some colored persons boasting of the white blood, but I always feel like blushing for mine."

When Louis finally discovers the truth of his origins, he quickly changes his politics and devotes himself to the cause of freedom and justice by fighting on the side of the Union Army. As a result of his experiences in the war, Louis espouses political principles that are a far cry from those he held when he believed himself to be a white southerner. But the question of the intermingling of the races in marriage is one that is of less interest here. "The question that presses upon us with the most fearful distinctness is how can we make life secure in the South. I sometimes feel as if the very air was busting with bayonets. There is no law here but the revolver. There must be a screw loose somewhere, and this government that taxes its men in peace and drafts them in war, ought to be wise enough to know its citizens and strong enough to protect them."[49] But, of course, the government is not wise. The government has little knowledge of its citizens and proves too weak to protect them from lynch mobs that wreak havoc against black Americans throughout the South following the war. Indeed, Louis and Minnie's happy marriage is tragically interrupted by her death, caused by an American government too weak to protect them from the forces of the Ku Klux Klan. After Minnie's death, Louis is more compelled than ever to continue the work they began together; after all, it was their mutual commitment to the work of uplifting the race that had brought them together in the first place. As Louis pictures Minnie's "shining robes and the radiant light of her glorified face" after her death, we realize that though their marriage ends with death, their work continues even after death.

Working through Marriage

To call the heroines of Harper's periodical fiction and the marriages she sets them in "ideal" is an understatement. Minnie, Belle, and Annette embody the unrealistic representation of black women that Mary Helen Washington has rightly dismissed in her introduction to *Black Eyed Susans,* as "some idealized nonsense about black women [that obstructs] real characters from whom we could learn more about ourselves." The radical implications of Harper's fiction are undercut when we consider that apart from Janette Alston, all of Harper's "self-reliant women" wind up married to ideal husbands. Veering away from the notion that marriage undercuts a woman's economic and emotional independence, she insists on rewarding women's self-restraint and virtue with a happy marriage. While some might view her fiction as undermining the hard-fought battle for women's rights, others view Harper's "model for female 'self-reliance'" more favorably. "For Harper," Hildegard Hoeller observes, "self-reliance implies both a sense of self and of solidarity with others."[50] The apparent tension in Harper's model of the self-reliant woman turns on the question of marriage in her fiction. Given the economic and legal constraints of marriage, wouldn't a marriage, even if it is to an ideal husband, undermine a woman's self-reliance? Distinguishing between white and black models of marriage in late-nineteenth-century America, historian Jacqueline Jones writes that the marriages of middle-class white women were "unproductive in the context of a cash-oriented, industrializing economy, and formally unable to take part in the nation's political process, they enjoyed financial security only insofar as their spouses were steady and reliable providers." Whereas white marriages of this period were considered unproductive and unequal, black marriages were the opposite. Jones continues, "In contrast, black working women in the South had a more equal relationship with their husbands in the sense that the two partners were not separated by extremes of economic power or political rights; black men and women lacked both."[51] In other words, it is precisely because nineteenth-century black Americans lacked rights that they found themselves in marriages that were, in Jones's terms, more equitable and happy. The logic of Jones's argument seems to make sense in light of Harper's fiction that concludes with women finding freedom through both work and marriage.

But it is also the case that marriage poses a great risk to their freedom. "I dare not run the fearful risk," Belle Gordon explains to the thoughtless Jeanette Roland, when she inquires why her cousin has "refused an excellent offer of marriage." Continuing the theme of "The Two Offers," *Sowing and Reaping* reiterates the scenario of female cousins contemplating marriage. More squarely focused on the question of temperance than on standing up for the downtrodden slave, *Sowing and Reaping* contrasts the lives of two women who take different paths. Whereas Jeanette claims to "take things as [she] find[s] them and drifts along the tide of circumstances," such a life does not suit Belle. "Life must mean to me more than ease, luxury and indulgence, it must mean aspiration and consecration, endeavor and achievement."[52] Given their different philosophies, it is no wonder that Jeanette believes Belle to have "thrown away a splendid opportunity" by breaking her engagement to the wealthy lawyer and occasional drinker Charles Romaine.

Much to both the reader's and Belle's surprise, she does marry in the end. When she receives a marriage proposal from Paul Clifford, she responds with shock and disbelief: "Your question was so unexpected and—." Here, Paul interrupts her in a tone of sad expectancy. "And what! . . . so unwelcome?" Belle does little to lift her suitor's sagging spirits. "It was so sudden, I was not prepared for it."[53] Leaving him with an ambivalent response—"I will think on it but for the present let us change the subject"—we believe that Belle will follow in the footsteps of the earlier Janette Alston.[54] Instead, we learn that Belle does in fact accept Paul's marriage proposal but only several chapters later. In the novel's final chapter, Harper informs readers that "life with Mrs. Clifford had become a thing of brightness and beauty . . . she was a wife and tender mother."[55] This is all well and good for the new Mrs. Clifford but seems to have little to do with the philosophy espoused by the former Belle Gordon.

Belle's marriage to Paul Clifford appears as something of an afterthought in a story that is far more preoccupied with the horrors of marriage. When Belle sets Charles free when she decides to break their engagement, her cousin wastes no time in picking up the pieces of his broken heart. Given their similar interests and tastes, the match seems like a suitable one. But like Laura Legrange of "The Two Offers," the marriage between Charles and Jeanette leads to the rapid decline of both, though Jeanette suffers more than her husband. As it happens, this is not the only example of an unhappy marriage, nor is it the most extreme case of one. Far worse is the case of John Anderson, a saloon owner, who marries a wealthy widow. The unhappy consequences of this union are the result of John's philosophy of women and marriage that he espouses proudly in his conversation with Paul Clifford with which the novel opens:

> I call her place staying at home and attending to her own affairs. Were I a laboring man I would never want my wife to take in work. When a woman has too much on hand, something has to be neglected. Now I always furnish my wife with sufficient help to supply every want but how I get the living, and where I go, and what company I keep, is my own business, and I would not allow the best woman in the world to interfere. I have often heard women say that they did not care what their husbands did, so that they provided for them; and I think such conclusions are very sensible.[56]

The conversation between Paul and John parallels that of Belle and Jeanette in the following chapter. John and Jeanette represent the wrong view of marriage while Paul and Belle espouse the right, though unpopular, view. John and Jeanette are like most people: They associate the institution of marriage with the stabilization of possessions. Both rely on marriage, rather than labor, to make a living. This is why John speaks of his own labor in the conditional tense—"were I a laboring man"—rather than in the present. John eventually decides to give up his grocery store and open a saloon because he rightly believes it will be more profitable. John understands that his occupation disqualifies him from the rank of a laboring man, making him instead a businessman, "a man who was almost destitute of faith in human goodness. His motto was that 'every man has his price.'"[57]

Drawing a direct and explicit connection between his business principles and his ideas about marriage, Harper spends almost two entire chapters of the story narrating the terms and consequences of his first broken engagement to a "young lady who taught school in his native village" and his eventual marriage to "a woman, who was no longer young in years, nor beautiful in person, nor amiable in temper. But she was rich, and her money like charity covered a multitude of faults."[58] Compared to the mere two paragraphs she devotes to Belle and Paul's happy marriage, Harper's attention to Jeanette and John's unhappy marriages suggests that the latter are more familiar and likely than are the former. Despite the negative association of marriage with money and greed, Harper shies away from denouncing marriage altogether. Instead, she removes it so far from reality that it appears to be nothing more than an unattainable, though desirable, ideal.

"It is nearly thirty years," Harper begins her 1892 address to the Brooklyn Literary Society, "since an emancipated people stood on the threshold of a new era, facing an uncertain future—a legally unmarried race to be taught the sacredness of the marriage relation."[59] These same words appear near the end of her novel, published the same year, to celebrate the end of slavery and the accomplishments of the formerly enslaved. Spoken by Iola's mother, the clever and beautiful Marie Leroy, they take on a different meaning in the context of the parlor conversation between "a select company of earnest men and women deeply interested in the welfare of the race."[60] Far removed from the "meetings [slaves] used to have in by-gone days," in "lonely woods and gloomy swamps," this meeting takes place among highly educated black men and women in a "well-lighted, beautifully-furnished room." Although the meeting functions for the novel's characters as a sign of "the wonderful changes that have come to us since the war," it is also a sign of a shift in Harper's position on marriage.[61]

There are no unhappy marriages in *Iola Leroy*. There are marriages between slaves, between a slave master and a female slave, between light-skinned blacks, and between a dark-skinned black woman and a light-skinned black man. Despite the differences in these marriages, they all are depicted as being happy unions. While the threat of an unhappy marriage still lingers in the form of Dr. Gresham's marriage proposal, Iola successfully avoids entering into a marriage that would give her "a palace-like home, with velvet carpets to hush my tread and magnificence to surround my way."[62] Iola instead chooses a marriage in which she will enjoy no such material advantages. Instead, she marries Dr. Latimer with whom she will be able "to stand on the threshold of a new era and labor for those who had passed from the old oligarchy of slavery into the new commonwealth of freedom."[63]

The near total absence of Harper's critique of marriage in *Iola Leroy*, articulated so forcefully in her periodical fiction, may project, as Gabrielle Foreman argues, "the volatile and violent unfolding of the 1890s."[64] Given the lynchings, sexual abuse, and sexual and political intimidation against black Americans that was characteristic of the decade, marriage seems as good a solution as any to defend and protect their fledgling sociopolitical status. But the marriage solution, as Harper makes clear in the closing chapters of the novel, is a solution only available to a select few, those like Iola and Dr. Latimer who have been blessed with a good education and light skin. Those not blessed with such good fortune must await the happy couple's counsel and example to touch their own lives since they remain "a legally unmarried race to be taught the sacredness of the marriage relation." Existing outside the legal constraints of marriage and without the material advantages Latimer and Iola enjoy, this group comes to symbolize a condition of pure labor: men and women who work for their living and are not distracted by the promise of wealth and social advancement that comes with a good marriage. It is only by wedding herself to this group first that Iola is able to enter into the kind of marriage that eluded Jeanette Alston and, indeed, Harper herself.

The opening chapters of *Iola Leroy*, Harper's final work of fiction that is set during the Civil War, locates marriage as essential to the slave community it presents. In recounting the story of his marriage to Aunt Katie, Uncle Daniel explains and justifies his decision not to join his fellow slaves in their efforts to become "contraband of war": "De fust time I seed her, I sez to myself, 'Dat's de gal for me, an' I means to hab her ef I kin git her.' So I scraped 'quaintance wid her, and axed her ef she would hab me ef our marsters would let us."[65] Uncle Daniel proceeds to recount their marriage, facilitated in large part by "Marse Robert's" efforts to keep the couple together despite the objections of Aunt Katie's owner. Because of his owner's successful efforts to protect their slave-marriage, Aunt Katie and Uncle Daniel, we are led to believe, do not need to run away since they are, in a sense, already free. When asked if she "feels bitter towards these people who are fighting to keep you in slavery," Aunt Katie "expressed the idea of a soul which had been fearfully tempest tossed, but had passed through suffering into peace."[66] The novel's singular slave-marriage serves the purpose not only of establishing the nature of the ties that bind the slaves together but also of providing a model of a marriage that works, and it is a model that Harper's heroine will eventually attempt to imitate through her marriage to Frank Latimer. After Iola and Latimer are married, they move to North Carolina where they are joined by the former slaves Aunt Linda and Uncle Daniel, who "was please to know that 'dat sweet young lady who had sich putty manners war comin' to lib wid dem."[67] By joining the newlyweds with the old slave couple, Harper concludes her novel with a post–slave community in which the younger generation teaches the older the ways of the New World, while the old imparts the knowledge of the slave past to the future generation. It is through this dialectic between slave and free marriage that her novel, unlike her short fiction, resolves the problem of marriage with which Harper grappled for much of her life.

5. Wedded to Race

Charles Chesnutt's *Stories of the Color Line*

Uncle Wellington, the title character of Charles W. Chesnutt's 1899 short story, "Uncle Wellington's Wives," must grapple with an unusual marital problem.[1] It is a problem absent from most nineteenth-century fictions regarding marriage, and yet it was confronted by thousands of those whom Chesnutt called "the newly emancipated race." Uncle Wellington learns from "the only colored lawyer in North Carolina" that Aunt Milly, the woman he had married when he was in slavery, or "befo' de wah," is not his "lawful wife."[2] The lawyer informs him that although Aunt Milly "may be [his] wife in one sense of the word," she is not so from a legal point of view. Without any legal ties binding him to Aunt Milly, Uncle Wellington is free to leave her. He anticipates material benefits from his leaving and even imagines some moral ones.

Along with the load of legal jargon the lawyer freely dispenses, he also advises Uncle Wellington not to act on his opportunity, "for [he has] a very good wife now."[3] But Uncle Wellington does not heed the lawyer's advice. The news has given him "a feeling of unaccustomed lightness and freedom. He had not felt so free since the memorable day when he had first heard of the Emancipation Proclamation."[4] However, that feeling of freedom is soon curtailed with his efforts to cross the color line by marrying a white woman in the North. Uncle Wellington learns that even though he is not legally married to Aunt Milly, he is bound to her by a force more powerful than "the sanction of law."[5] Their attachment, based upon their shared experience of slavery, is less concrete but more profound than the terms of a legal marriage.

"Uncle Wellington's Wives" is one of the nine stories in Chesnutt's short-story collection *The Wife of His Youth and Other Stories of the Color Line*

(1899). As its title suggests, the collection is distinguished by the connections between slavery, race, and marriage that Uncle Wellington's "matrimonial experiences" exemplify. Like Uncle Wellington, the characters of Chesnutt's *Stories of the Color Line* exhibit a remarkable ignorance regarding the laws and conventions of marriage that are the inevitable consequence of slavery. Chesnutt's stories function, at least in part, as a way of illustrating the significance of marriage to former slaves and their descendants—those who, as Ann duCille points out, "for generations were denied the hegemonic, 'universal truth' of legal marriage."[6]

Marriage, Uncle Wellington learns by abandoning his slave wife to pursue greater wealth and social status in the North, is partly, and yet not simply, a matter of individual freedom and choice. If multitudes of former slaves were to choose their marriage partners so as to cross the color line, the line itself would be eliminated over generations. But if the same choice were made merely by an individual or a subset of former slaves, the result would be, at best, frustration and lack of progress. As Uncle Wellington finds, the individual's marriage choice may incite discrimination by observers from the other side of the color line should he attempt to cross it. Alternatively, as Chesnutt illustrates in other *Stories of the Color Line*, an intraracial color line, dividing light-skinned blacks who have the option of intermarriage from the dark-skinned blacks who do not, may be substituted for the interracial one.

Yet the latter possibilities are not the only ones representing how, to Chesnutt, the newly won freedom of marriage is qualified by unsettling consequences. Nor are they even the most notable ones. When former slaves decide not to cross the line with their marriage choices—opting instead to secure and protect relationships formed before the war, and thus to demonstrate loyalty, honor, and fidelity to their slave pasts and commitment to race—Chesnutt suggests that the outcome is no better. In fact, Chesnutt casts a surprisingly critical eye on the movement to legitimate slave-marriages during Reconstruction, a movement celebrated by historians of marriage and slavery alike. Instead, Chesnutt views "the freed people who had sustained to each other the relation of husband and wife as it existed among slaves, [as being] *required by law* to register their consent to continue in the marriage relation. By this simple expedient their former marriages of convenience received the sanction of law" (italics added).[7] Offering slave-marriages "the sanction of law" functioned as a powerful incentive for former slaves to maintain marriages that were formed without consent. Such decisions inscribe an essential difference between black and white forms of marriage, since the former signifies a connection to slavery. Chesnutt's Uncle Wellington offers a noteworthy, albeit fictional, example of a former slave who follows a different course from that prescribed by the law. The results of Uncle Wellington's matrimonial experiences suggest that, with or without consent, marriage does not bring the slave the freedom promised by Reconstruction. The following examination of Chesnutt's fiction and criticism suggests that the unhappy consequences of making race essential to marital consent in the Reconstruction era was a problem on both sides of the color line.

Uncle Wellington's Reconstruction

Compared with the preeminent rights that slaves were denied—the right to vote and to own their bodies and labor—the denial of their right to marry was of less transcendent, yet more immediate, importance.[8] The Fourteenth and Fifteenth Amendments, after all, guaranteed equality and enfranchisement but did not make them operational. Legal marriage guaranteed less but delivered more. Registration of their marriages enabled former slaves to maintain familial and intimate connections that were often broken by the slave system. It made inheritance possible, and so held out the prospect of the accumulation of wealth and social status. Reconstruction efforts thus included reuniting families that had been broken by slavery and making slave-marriages legal.[9] Historian Nancy Cott argues that such efforts were essential for securing national peace and stability following the turmoil caused by slavery and the Civil War. "Where 'barbarism' and 'unbridled licentiousness' had flourished," Cott writes, "national honor, dignity and morality had to be restored, and could be so only through marriage."[10]

However, to legitimize by marriage what duCille has helpfully called "the coupling convention" of former slaves was not without cost. Uncle Wellington understood the cost well. When emancipation was proclaimed, former slaves beheld the prospect of liberty and perhaps even equality and full privileges of citizenship. But the prospect's realization required more than a proclamation and change of law. The vestiges of bondage and inequality would have to be dismantled; the importance of color would have to be diminished. To cement relations that were formed in bondage would reconstruct, as it were, that which required dismantling; to produce offspring from those relations would retrace, not efface, the color line. Perhaps national honor, dignity, and privileges such as legal inheritance would indeed be gained by legitimizing the couplings, but liberty, equality, and privileges of citizenship would be sacrificed.

That former slaves might make the sacrifice willingly, with regret for having to choose but not for their choice, preoccupied Chesnutt. For Chesnutt, legitimizing slave-marriages supplemented the move to prohibit "the marriage relation between white persons and persons of African descent" by making race, rather than economic considerations or perhaps even love, determine intimate relations. Thus Uncle Wellington decides after ending his marriage to Aunt Milly, and before returning to her, that the "[l]iberty, equality, privileges" he imagined awaited him in the North "all were but as dust in the balance when weighed against his longing for old scenes and faces."[11] In the end, Uncle Wellington's attempt to follow the program of racial uplift proscribed by the slick Professor Patterson, whose lecture on "The Mental, Moral, Physical, Social, and Financial Improvement of the Negro Race in America" leads Uncle Wellington to believe that social equality might be achieved by espousing a white woman in the North, fails miserably. Realizing "that he had been a great fool,"[12] he returns to the South with a greater appreciation for its virtues and devotion to the woman who "ain't [his] lawful wife."[13]

Chesnutt treats the connection between Uncle Wellington's former slave experiences and his current matrimonial experiences with a good deal of irony, the rhetorical mode characterizing his preoccupation with marriage in *Stories of the Color Line*. By recounting experiences of love and intimacy with a certain ironic distance, we are in a better position to comprehend the ethical or affective, and therefore voluntary, dimension of racial divisions. The same cannot be said of all his works, even though the connections between marriage, slavery, and race are common to all of them.[14] Critics have tended to focus on those of Chesnutt's works emphasizing the importance of historical and legal constraints to intermarriage that reflect his related, and yet different, concern with the compulsory dimension of Reconstruction.

The complex role marriage plays in Chesnutt's stories of the color line confounds its readers. Engaged in the literary conventions of the marriage plots, Chesnutt's characters find themselves trapped within a fiction of race that prevents them from achieving the happy endings typical of the marriage plot. The tension between the conventions of race and marriage central to Chesnutt's plots make his stories difficult to categorize. Read as "a fiction of manners," in which characters are forced to confront color prejudices in their efforts to comply with the rituals of courtship and marriage, Chesnutt's fiction dramatizes, as Nancy Bentley explains, "the stakes of civil marriage in a post slavery era."[15] The didactic element found in much of Chesnutt's fiction sets it apart, according to recent critics, from the school of American literary realism that marks Chesnutt's contemporary era. Emphasizing the importance of the historical conditions informing much of Chesnutt's fiction, critics have tended to focus on his novel *The Marrow of Tradition*, which provides a fictional account of the organized violence against black citizens living in Wilmington, North Carolina, in 1898. Chesnutt's fictional rendering of this historical event bears a vital connection to Webb's novel *The Garies and Their Friends*. Unlike Webb's work, however, Chesnutt's concludes on a far less optimistic note concerning the future of the black middle class.

The romantic elements of Chesnutt's *Stories of the Color Line* and his first novel, *The House behind the Cedars* (1900), have become mere sidebars to the critique of race Chesnutt provides in his historical fiction. Critics in search of historical truth have little interest in his fictional romances aimed at dissolving the color line that prevents his characters from attaining the happily-ever-after ending of the marriage plot. In Chesnutt's stories of the color line, a character's belief in race conflicts with romantic conventions, making it impossible for his relationship to end happily with marriage. The narrative disruptions that marriage causes break the unity conventionally associated with marriage, revealing the principles of the segregation plot that constitutes the most enduring aspect of Chesnutt's oeuvre. In Chesnutt's segregation plot, marriage is regulated by racial principles and prejudices that result in two separate but equal definitions of marriage. Marriage is based on love and consent if you are white, but on a commitment to race if you are not. For this reason, Chesnutt's *Stories of the Color Line* end tragically; the happy endings associated with the conventional marriage plot always elude Chesnutt's protagonists.

The marriage problem, as Chesnutt presents it in *The Marrow of Tradition*, centers on the criminalization of intermarriage.[16] A certificate of marriage signifies not only a binding union between consenting adults, but it may also be evidence of "some terrible crime" punishable by fines and even imprisonment. Although criminalization of intermarriage is also present in *Stories of the Color Line*, it is not a central theme. Uncle Wellington's marriage to a white woman, for instance, is legal but the attitudes against their marriage prove too great for the interracial couple to overcome. When Uncle Wellington consults a lawyer about dissolving his second, but first legal, marriage, he is subjected to a new form of racial prejudice: "[I]t's what you might have expected when you turned your back on your own people and married a white woman."[17] Uncle Wellington's belief that his lighter skin entitles him to "a much higher sphere in life than that in which the accident of birth had placed him" leads only to folly and misadventure.[18] His desire to leave his slave wife and marry a white woman in the North betrays not only the terms of his slave-marriage but also his "own people." Voluntary constraints are more relevant to the *Stories of the Color Line* than the involuntary ones; those that are imposed from within the race are more binding than those imposed from without. When the color line is redrawn continually from both sides, black and white, it is less provocative of violence than in the alternative case but is also a more tractable problem. As such, Chesnutt insists, it is at least equally worthy of attention.

Professor Patterson, and the irony that attends his prescription and the paltry results it achieves, is to be read as a reflection of Chesnutt's skepticism that the problem can be easily overcome by intermarriage, but not as an endorsement of the alternative of the voluntary eschewal of intermarriage. To the contrary, in Uncle Wellington one sees the costs of that approach. The emphasis on those costs, and yet also an ironic detachment from those who would seem to proffer an alternative, are equally evident in other *Stories of the Color Line*.

"The Wife of His Youth"

The first, and most famous, of Chesnutt's *Stories of the Color Line* is the title story, "The Wife of His Youth," which relates the effects of a slave-marriage on the life of an individual who is committed to erasing his past slave experiences in order to make a future for himself as a free man. As a young man, Mr. Ryder had fled north to escape slavery. After the Civil War, he rose to a position of eminence in the "light-colored" community and devoted himself to elevating its status.[19] As the leader of the community—the "dean of the Blue Veins"—Mr. Ryder's character personifies its values. His purpose, as Chesnutt describes it, "was to establish and maintain correct social standards among a people whose social condition presented almost unlimited room for improvement."[20]

The story's action centers on Mr. Ryder's efforts to find a wife who shares his social principles and "literary tastes" and meets his "economical" interests as well. Molly Dixon wins Mr. Ryder's heart by possessing the necessary "qualities."[21] Their match appears to be inevitable as they both play leading roles in the activities of the Blue Veins. Mr. Ryder's plan to marry Mrs. Dixon is interrupted by the appearance of Liza Jane, a woman who "looked like a bit of the old plantation life, summoned up from the past by the wave of the magician's wand."[22] Mr. Ryder must choose between his past marriage with a former slave, a woman who risked her own life to save his, and a woman who "moved in the best colored society of the country."[23]

Before Liza Jane's appearance, Mr. Ryder displays little capacity for romance. Aside from his passion for poetry, Mr. Ryder is a model of bourgeois virtue: "He was economical, and had saved money; he owned and occupied a very comfortable house on a respectable street."[24] Following his conservative tastes and role as a "preserver of traditions," Mr. Ryder approaches marriage rationally. Mr. Ryder's desire to make Molly Dixon his wife conforms to the middle-class values he so faithfully observes. But the appearance of the wife of his youth upsets those values; Liza Jane's blackness, manifested not only by the color of her wrinkled skin and "toothless gums" but also by the ancient clothes she wears and her "old-fashioned brass brooch," interrupts Mr. Ryder's progressive middle-class narrative of wealth and happiness by forcing him to remember where he came from.[25]

The tension surrounding Mr. Ryder's decision has most often been read in terms of his "mixed" racial identity. The story's "central character," Charles Duncan explains, "must confront his own past in determining whether he can reconcile his urge to 'advance' his race with his family duty."[26] Like Uncle Wellington, Mr. Ryder's marital decision is read as an allegory for the "mulatto" subject who must choose between black and white racial identities, realizing, in the end, that choosing to be black—by maintaining his commitment to his slave wife—is the right thing to do, even though it involves giving up Molly Dixon and the middle-class life he has worked so hard to attain. In contrast to the "many attractive qualities" Molly Dixon possesses, Liza Jane embodies certain intangible virtues, namely "devotion," "confidence," "faith," and "affection,"[27] that in the end are more highly prized than Molly Dixon's white skin, youth, education, and considerable fortune.[28]

The foregoing allegorical reading of "The Wife of His Youth" is complicated, as Henry Wonham recently explained, by the "anti-race" position Chesnutt articulates elsewhere. Well-known nonfiction essays such as "What Is a White Man?" and the three-part series on "The Future American" evinces Chesnutt's belief that "amalgamation" of the races will bring an inevitable— and desirable—end to racial identification.[29] Departing from the anti-amalgamationist or black separatist positions represented in the works of other nineteenth-century African American novels—those by Frank Webb, Frances Harper, and Sutton Griggs—Chesnutt understands amalgamation not just as a mixture of the races but as an end to the very idea of racial difference. In order to understand the significance of Chesnutt's position, we have to leap from his fiction to his criticism in which he discusses, under the guise of objective distance, the problem with laws prohibiting intermarriage.

Chesnutt explains that "[w]hatever the wisdom or justice of these laws, there is one objection to them which is not given sufficient prominence in the consideration of the subject, even where it is discussed at all; they make mixed blood a *prima-facie* proof of illegitimacy." The essay is further instructive because it helps to define people of "mixed blood." The irony of their position is that they threaten to upset racial distinctions while at the same time proving indispensable in upholding those very same distinctions.

Given the choice to be black or white, the rational decision would be to be white. The fact that certain laws have been instituted to prevent people of mixed blood from behaving rationally shows, according to Chesnutt, the irrational nature of those who institute those "black laws" that regulate "the relations of the races."[30] By declaring the law irrational, Chesnutt promotes the individual's desire to act according to his self-interest.

Yet self-interest is precisely what Mr. Ryder abandons in "The Wife of His Youth." His decision to do so is often valorized by Chesnutt's readers today.[31] Nevertheless, Chesnutt himself makes clear that the decision is driven by an archaic, but no less compelling, notion of "honor" and justice, and more to the point, tied to an irrational understanding of race. Although Mr. Ryder recounts his story to his audience with the impartiality and distance of a third-person narrator, "[t]here was something in Mr. Ryder's voice that stirred the hearts of those who sat around him," his voice betrays a personal investment that interferes with his ability to behave "impartially."[32]

And yet, to observe that Mr. Ryder's decision is a troubling one for Chesnutt is not to say that the most evident alternative for him, and much less for the Blue Veins in general, is untroubled. As in his ironic portrayal of Uncle Wellington's misguided decision to abandon Aunt Milly in order to find a white wife in the North, the social principles the Blue Veins manifest are subject to Chesnutt's biting social criticism. The Blue Veins see themselves as members of a growing black middle class committed to putting the experiences and associations of slavery behind them. To the chagrin of the author, however, their class affiliation is inflected by race. "By accident, combined perhaps with some natural affinity, the society consisted of individuals who were, generally speaking, more white than black."[33] The problem with the Blue Veins, then, is not in the exclusiveness they so openly practice but rather that they exclude on the basis of race rather than class. "The Wife of His Youth" ultimately exposes the problem with conflating race and class. Against the practice of the Blue Veins, Chesnutt's story maintains, these two aspects of social life should be kept separate. Not doing so results in confusion and, as in the case of Mr. Ryder, a loss of identity and social status.

The Future of Marriage

When "The Wife of His Youth" was first published in the July 1898 issue of the *Atlantic Monthly*, it met with rave reviews from critics and readers alike. One reviewer summed up the story's virtues by exclaiming that it is "marvelously simple, touching and fascinating."[34] After having experienced a series of blows to his efforts to publish literary fiction, Chesnutt received the affirmative response to "The Wife of His Youth" at a critical moment in his literary career. In a letter to his editor, Walter Hines Page, Chesnutt expressed the importance of the story in helping him to establish his credentials as an author. He writes, "I have been hearing from my story every day since its publication. . . . I have had letters from my friends and notices in all the local papers . . . and taking it all in all, I have had a slight glimpse of what it means, I imagine, to be a successful author."[35] The moral dilemma Chesnutt's story presents seems to have helped him transcend certain racial barriers. Significantly, "The Wife of His Youth" was the first work of fiction by a black author to appear in the pages of the much-esteemed *Atlantic Monthly*.

However, that success, as Chesnutt would soon realize, came at a cost. Despite all the accolades heaped upon "The Wife of His Youth," Chesnutt was troubled by misreadings of the story that undermined its message. "It is surprising," Chesnutt later wrote to Page, "that a number of people do not seem to imagine that the old woman was entitled to any consideration whatever and yet I don't know that it is so astonishing either, in the light of history."[36] While Chesnutt's mostly white contemporary readers were surprised by Mr. Ryder's choice, more recent interpretations suggest the opposite response. Liza Jane has thus emerged as the story's hero "for her *womanly* 'fidelity and devotion to those she loves.'"[37] We might understand the divergence between these interpretations as sharing Mr. Ryder's racial commitments.

"The Wife of His Youth" presents the commitment to race as a historical fiction: not just as a chronology of past events but also as a recollection of them that his characters desire unconsciously to reproduce in the present. In Chesnutt's terms, the affective dimension of history is more powerful than most of us imagine; it has the capacity to threaten progress and stifle growth. Based upon Chesnutt's sense of history, his fiction is devoted to exposing its effects on the life of the individual. Ultimately, Chesnutt's stories narrate the ways in which the personal commitment to life before the Civil War makes it impossible to tell a free story in postbellum America.

It is perhaps not surprising that Chesnutt expressed his critique of history in the form of social criticism rather than fiction. In this mode, Chesnutt presents a program for the future in the guise of objectivity, without having to account for the effects of history on its subjects and the sentiments of characters constrained by it. These essays are not about people, black or white; they are preoccupied instead by laws, numbers, and blood. Presenting marriage in the language of scientific reason rather than sentimental fiction offers a novel view of the subject. While Reconstruction politicians and activists advocated marriage as essential to reuniting former slaves and securing the "liberty, equality and privileges" that they were denied during slavery, Chesnutt presents marriage as a way of dismantling relations formed by slavery. In a series of essays published in 1900 for the *Boston Transcript*, Chesnutt provides what he calls a "mechanical" solution to the race problem that radically revises the conventions of love and consent distinguishing marriage.[38] The revolution that Chesnutt's "Future American" essay outlines is based upon doing away with racial divisions by creating a single "American race" through the reproductive potential of marriage:

> Taking the population as one-eighth Negro, this eighth, married to an equal number of whites, would give in the next generation a population of which one-fourth would be mulattoes. Mating these in turn with white persons, the next generation would be composed one-half of quadroons, or persons one-fourth Negro. In the third generation, applying the same rule, the entire population would be composed of octoroons, or persons only one-eighth Negro, who would probably call themselves white, if by this time there remained any particular advantage in being so considered. Thus in three generations the pure whites would be entirely eliminated and there would be no perceptible trace of the blacks left.[39]

What does this belief in numbers, in an arithmetic solution to the race problem, signify? How would such a solution present a viable alternative to "the vulgar theory of race"?[40] By making marriage a simple matter of adding a certain number of "Negroes" to an equal number of "whites," Chesnutt reveals the absurdity of making marriage a matter of race, rather than mutual desire and love. Making marriage conform to certain racial or "black laws" rather than what Chesnutt calls "natural laws" radically alters the principles of marriage. Marriage constitutes a free and consensual union of two people. By echoing the discourse of racial eugenics so popular at the time, Chesnutt's theory suggests creating a singular, superior "American race" by which "a government sufficiently autocratic to enforce its behests" will be able to eliminate the distinction between black and white. However desirable a future without any trace of racial difference may be, Chesnutt readily admits that his marital solution to America's race problem "will never happen."[41] Marriage, for Chesnutt at least, should not be regulated by others; it should be a matter of individual choice and consent. Chesnutt's essay reviles those governments and individuals who interfere with the natural laws of marriage.

Chesnutt's "scientific fiction" of a future American race bears a striking resemblance to the fantastic and absurd discovery Ralph Ellison's protagonist stumbles upon as an employee of Liberty Paints. In *Invisible Man*, we learn that the purity of the Optic White paint, which also goes by the name Right White, can only be produced by stirring exactly ten drops of "dead black" paint with white. Like Ellison's protagonist, Chesnutt's theory of race suggests that underlying all notions of racial purity is the idea of mixture. Whereas Ellison's protagonist comes to understand how racial difference is produced by the combination of specific chemicals, Chesnutt employs the word "race" in his theory of the future only in its "popular sense," conceding that the term holds no scientific meaning or truth value. For Chesnutt, as for Ellison, race is a pure fiction, something that is invented in an imaginary factory by men wearing white suits. For Chesnutt, race is merely genealogical (a matter of who one's ancestors are), and its power is lessened by giving everyone the same ancestry. It is precisely because race lacks any "real" meaning that Chesnutt believes it can "disappear" by making people believe that intermarriage would put an end to "the elements of racial discord which have troubled our civil life so gravely and still threaten free institutions."[42]

The point of the essay, and of Chesnutt's fiction in general, is to show how the commitment to race distorts the conventions of marriage. "So ferocious is this sentiment against intermarriage," Chesnutt laments, "that in a recent Missouri case, where a colored man ran away with and married a young white woman, the man was pursued by a 'posse' . . . and shot to death."[43] The couple, in this instance, are clearly in love, so in love that they are willing to risk their lives in order to be together. But that love makes no difference to a "posse" dead set against their union. This posse acts in direct concert with "proscriptive legislation" that similarly interferes with the natural laws regulating love and marriage.

Whether Chesnutt's readers denounce his vision of the future as a "theory [that] implicitly celebrates white skin" or extol it "as a kind of utopian solution to a problem that seemed otherwise intractable," they all foreground "race" as the key component of the essay.[44] But race is secondary to Chesnutt's theory; its first priority is imagining a future in which racial divisions have disappeared. To imagine this disappearance, Chesnutt's fiction demands that we first rethink the meaning of marriage. Marriage is about making a promise to the future, a promise that should effect a break with the past. For some, like Liza Jane, marriage ties us to the place where we came from; for others, like Mr. Ryder and Uncle Wellington, marriage has the potential to take us far away from the old scenes and faces of our origins. As it turns out, both ideas of marriage are not without its flaws.

The antiracial act *par excellence* that emblematizes, in Chesnutt's fiction, both a future without race and the commitment to a racial past is the repetitive violation of the institution of marriage. Nowhere is this violation made more apparent than in the climax of what critics have called Chesnutt's major novel of segregation, *The Marrow of Tradition*.[45] Detailing the events leading up to a violent race riot, Chesnutt's novel occupies a central position in the African American literary canon. The novel's importance for current conceptions of the canon lies in its retelling of an infamous race riot. The violence the novel represents is the consequence of the racial logic underlying the enactment of the "separate but equal" principle articulated by the Supreme Court in *Plessy v. Ferguson*. The novel depicts the progress of two families—the Cartarets and the Millers—one white, one black, who would be a single family if not for the "arbitrary" color line that divides them. *The Marrow of Tradition* imagines the color line as a fiction cooked up by a cabal of Southern white men, led by Major Cartaret, who find common cause in their perceived threat of "negro domination."[46] In stark contrast to the "fiction" of the color line is the "reality" of the marriage certificate. Interestingly, the fiction of the color line is associated with the novel's white male characters, whereas marriage is presented as the purview of women. It is through Cartaret's wife, Olivia, that the novel articulates its position on marriage and how the terms it establishes for intimacy are a vital supplement to the rhetoric of the color line.

The color line appears in full force in the novel's opening chapters and helps to frame the introduction of the novel's chief black character and hero, Dr. William Miller. Miller is distinguished not by the color of his skin, which happens to be "a light brown," but by the "health and prosperity" he embodies. We meet Miller on a southbound train from Philadelphia where he notices the presence of a former friend and colleague, Dr. Burns, who is headed to North Carolina to perform an operation on Major Cartaret's only son. The chance meeting between the two doctors on the train leads to one of the most memorable scenes of racial segregation in literary fiction. The conversation between them is interrupted by the train's conductor who insists that they separate to comply with "the law of Virginia [that] does not permit colored passengers to ride in the white cars."[47] This scene dramatizes the circumstances that led to the Supreme Court's decision in *Plessy v. Ferguson*. As is well known, the plaintiff in the case, Homer Adolph Plessy, argued that the segregation laws prohibiting him from sitting in the "Whites Only" car of the train denied him his constitutional rights guaranteed by the Thirteenth and Fourteenth Amendments. But the argument Miller makes against segregation is a slightly different one. When approached by the conductor, Miller insists that he has paid his fare on the sleeping car "where the separate-car law does not apply."[48] His ability to pay the proper fare, in other words, gives him the right to sit in the white car. But Miller's economic logic is easily refuted by the conductor's racial logic. "But this is a day coach," he responds, "and is distinctly marked 'White,' as you must have seen before you sat down here."[49] Of course Miller had seen the sign, but he "had hoped on account of his friend's presence" that such an altercation "might be avoided."[50] Miller soon learns that a friendship between a white doctor and a black doctor is not enough to undo the laws of segregation: "It is the law, and we are powerless to resist it."[51]

In his failed attempts to continue his conversation with Miller, Dr. Burns repeatedly cites Miller's "rights" to remain in the white car. "You shall stay right here," he instructs Miller and then, turning to the conductor, explains, "And my friend has his rights to maintain. . . . There is a vital principle at stake in the matter." Seeing that his invocation of rights and principles are no match for the law when the conductor dispassionately informs him that "the law gives me the right to remove him by force," Dr. Burns loses not just the argument but also his temper. "This is a d___d outrage! You are curtailing the rights, not only of colored people, but of white men as well. I shall sit where I please!"[52] But Burns's blustery rhetoric of rights has little effect. The scene concludes without violence and a passive acceptance of the laws of segregation, which prove too powerful for even a man of Burns's racial and class status to overcome: "Dr. Burns, finding resistance futile, at length acquiesced and made for Miller to pass him."[53] Segregation is a legal matter and yet has little to do with what is right. The language of rights Burns employs to persuade the conductor only frustrates him, leaving both men entirely at the mercy of the law. But this is only the beginning of the story. At the heart of the novel lies a secret history of a family romance that, when finally revealed through Cartaret's wife, Olivia, has the power to change the hearts and minds of those who believe that segregation is right.

Olivia finds herself in possession of her father's marriage certificate to a former slave whom he married after the death of her mother. This certificate renders the ideology of white supremacy that structures not only her life but also the lives of all those around her to be absolutely false. To deal with the shock of her discovery, Olivia destroys the marriage certificate. But the flames that consume the document do not diminish its meaning: "As the days wore on, Mrs. Cartaret grew still less at ease. To herself marriage was a serious thing—to a right-thinking woman the most serious concern of life. A marriage certificate, rightfully procured, was scarcely less solemn, so far as it went, than the Bible itself. Her own she cherished as the apple of her eye. It was the evidence of her wifehood, the seal of her child's legitimacy, her patent of nobility—the token of her own and her child's claim to social place and consideration."[54] Just as Dr. Burns invokes the rhetoric of rights to argue against Virginia law, Olivia sees herself as a "right-thinking woman" who understands marriage as a right that protects her white privilege. But the marriage between her white father, Mr. Merkell, and his black servant, Julia

Brown, and their child, Janet Miller, undermines that privilege. To protect her "rights," Olivia has no choice but to destroy the marriage certificate, thereby depriving Janet of her rightful inheritance as the legitimate daughter of their father. While considering herself to be a "right-thinking woman," Olivia's actions reveal something about marriage that those who view it as essential to the slave's freedom consistently neglect to mention: Marriage sanctifies some couples at the expense of others and is predicated upon selective legitimacy. "This," as Michael Warner reminds us, "is a necessary implication of the institution."[55]

The marriage certificate is like the Bible insofar as it is a document that has the power to convert or change the status of those it engages. But this marriage certificate has no legal effect. By destroying the certificate, Olivia believes she has not only "removed all traces of her dead father's folly" but also protected him from being implicated in a crime. "The marriage of white and colored persons was forbidden by law. Only recently she had read of a case where both the parties to such a crime, a colored man and a white woman, had been sentenced to long terms in the penitentiary."[56] Olivia finds herself torn between legal and filial duties. The law, as her husband explains to her, would not recognize the union between her father and a former slave, even if the certificate had been preserved. Like the will he leaves behind recognizing the daughter of his union with a black woman as his legitimate heir, the certificate legally as well as morally has "no effect." Although the public meaning of marriage is foreclosed by Olivia's actions, she has no control, Chesnutt makes clear, over its private meaning. "She had destroyed the marriage certificate," Chesnutt writes, "but its ghost still haunted her."[57]

Olivia's efforts to destroy or erase her father's marriage and the existence of her half-sister, Janet Miller, backfire terribly. The novel concludes with a confrontation between the sisters. Olivia begs forgiveness for her past sins and finally acknowledges her father's daughter as her sister. "Listen, sister!" she said. "I have a confession to make. You *are* my lawful sister. My father was married to your mother. You are entitled to his name, and to half his estate."[58] But that recognition does not change the meaning of Janet's life: "You imagined that the shame of being a negro swallowed up every other ignominy—and in your eyes, I am a negro."[59] In the end, Olivia and Janet both find themselves wedded to the color line by marriage. "Now, when an honest man has given me a name of which I can be proud, you offer me the one which you robbed me, and of which I can make no use."[60] In other words, the laws of segregation and marriage appear to be one and the same. Olivia initially refuses to recognize the union between her father and Janet's mother because she believes such a union to be against the law; she thus destroys the marriage certificate to protect her inheritance as her father's only legitimate heir. Acknowledging Janet as her sister would result in "a division of her father's estate" and "a scandal Mrs. Cartaret could not have endured."[61] Olivia only acknowledges her sister in order to "save her child [for that] she would shrink at no sacrifice."[62] By the time Olivia is forced to recognize Janet, however, the damage has already been done. The belief in the legitimacy of marriage has ultimately bound both women, even more tightly than the laws of segregation separating men on trains, to their race.

A Story of Us

Why exactly did former slaves and government officials go to the trouble of registering marriages if, as Liza Jane explains in her distinctive slave voice, such legal recognition "would n make no diff'ence" to her bond "wid Sam"?[63] Historians explain that marriage was integral to, as Amy Dru Stanley writes, "the passage from slavery to contract." According to this view, marriage is no different from labor contracts that made slaves into free subjects; registering slave-marriages thus protected the "sanctity of contract."[64] However, here I would like to displace, or at least add to, the findings of historical analysis in order to bring to bear upon them the sentiments and desires of the newly freed that Chesnutt's stories represent. Marriage, in Chesnutt's fiction, signifies not only personal choice and the capacity to enter into a contract; it is also the means by which a postslavery racial community is formed. While historians typically view marriage as key to the transition from slavery to freedom, Chesnutt reveals it as a tool of segregation, an aspect of segregation that goes well beyond designating racial divisions between public spaces; marriage, in Chesnutt's postslavery fiction, functions as the means by which racial distinctions are preserved.

The equality promised by the laws of segregation is, as Chesnutt demonstrates throughout his literary career, a promise that is repeatedly broken. The broken promise of segregation is the structuring principle of Chesnutt's *Stories of the Color Line*. Departing from the tone of nostalgia characterizing his earlier collection of short stories, *The Conjure Woman* (1899), Chesnutt's *Stories of the Color Line* remains focused on the conditions and problems confronting the "present generation." The difference between these collections has often been read as "an emblem of Chesnutt's divided sensibilities."[65] However, such criticism neglects the connection between the two collections; *Stories of the Color Line* supplements and extends the slave fictions narrated by Uncle Julius in *The Conjure Woman*. Through the unifying voice of Uncle Julius, the old days of slavery are presented as a romantic fiction. No such unifying presence exists in *Stories of the Color Line*. Instead, Chesnutt presents the effects of the slave fictions Uncle Julius recounts on the scattered lives of the present generation. Uncle Julius's stories of slavery have little to do with his actual experiences as a slave; instead, they reveal what Chesnutt calls "the simple but intensely human inner life of slavery."[66] It is this inner life, or affective dimension, of slavery that produces the idea of racial difference in the present and one to which Chesnutt's characters, for better or for worse, remain committed.

Through fiction, Chesnutt reveals the terms by which racial intimacies develop between the teller and listener of a story. By revealing the structures of racial intimacy, Chesnutt's fiction wavers between maintaining the bonds of those intimacies and leaving them behind to pursue an uncertain future. In "The Wife of His Youth," the relation between Mr. Ryder and Liza Jane develops when he invites her to tell him her story. As she tells her story, Chesnutt provides bits of information about how it is being received by her listener. Liza Jane relates her story in a distinct vernacular voice that interrupts the story by Alfred Lord Tennyson that Mr. Ryder had been reading when she entered. The formal differences between the two love stories affect Mr. Ryder in kind. While he experiences "an appreciative thrill"[67] reading Tennyson, he merely looks "curiously [at Liza Jane] when she finished."[68] Mr. Ryder does not seem to know how to respond to her story, so far removed is he from the experiences she relates. As a result, he questions both the teller's authority and the facts she relates. "Do you really expect to find your husband? He may be dead long ago."[69] To which Liza Jane "shook her head emphatically."[70] Liza Jane's unequivocal responses to Mr. Ryder's questions and the hard evidence she provides to justify the claims she makes eventually diminish his disbelief and force him to admire "such devotion and confidence [which] are rare even among women."[71] Liza Jane's story produces a change in her listener that forces him to see himself in the image of the man Liza Jane has devoted her life to finding.

But Mr. Ryder does not become that man until he retells Liza Jane's story "in the same soft dialect" himself. Interestingly, when Mr. Ryder tells the story, "the company listened attentively and sympathetically"; he produced in his listeners an aesthetic response previously associated with Mr. Ryder's reading of Tennyson's poem: "For the story awakened a responsive thrill in many hearts. There were some present who had seen, and others who had heard their father and grandfather tell the wrongs and suffering of this past generation, and all of them still felt, in their darker moments, the shadow hanging over them."[72] The story Mr. Ryder tells is not exactly a love story; it is something deeper and "darker" that does not conclude with the happy marriage of the story's central male and female characters. This story is as much about the listeners as it is about the characters involved in the action; it is a story about how slavery makes them feel and how slavery experienced by their parents and grandparents controls the most intimate aspects of their lives.

In the ethical relation between teller and listener that the story develops, Mr. Ryder is compelled to choose, in Werner Sollors's useful formulation, descent (acceptance of inherited categories based on race) over consent (choice of culture defined outside inherited ethnic or racial boundaries). "The Wife of His Youth" ends with Mr. Ryder's sense of honor intact but leaves readers wondering whether or not he has done the right thing. Was the old woman *really* entitled to such consideration, as the story's first readers complained? Or should Mr. Ryder have chosen Molly Dixon in order to effect his definitive break with a past that he had long left behind? Should he be responsible for Liza Jane's deluded belief that the reunion of the former slaves would enable them to "be as happy in freedom as we wuz in de old days befo' de wah"? Or might it be impossible to be as happy in freedom as Liza Jane claims they were in slavery? In order to keep a promise he made during slavery, Mr. Ryder is compelled to abandon his middle-class pursuits and comply with the racial injunction of his fellow Blue Veins: "He should have acknowledged her." Readers are left to ponder the implications of Mr. Ryder's decision for the desires of this budding black middle-class community to which he once so proudly belonged.

Chesnutt's Marriage Plots

While the slave-marriage lacks legal recognition, it nonetheless is deemed preferable to the much-anticipated legal marriage between Mr. Ryder and Molly Dixon. The important role the community plays in determining Mr. Ryder's marital decision is, of course, inherent to the institution of marriage itself. "To *be* marriage," Cott explains, "the institution requires public affirmation."[73] In this case, however, public affirmation is not just a question of silently witnessing a union. This community is granted the power of speech and, as a result, plays an active role in determining the outcome of Mr. Ryder's choice. Given his racial affiliation, Mr. Ryder's marriage is neither a matter of personal desire nor mutual love. The choice between Liza Jane and Molly Dixon is one Mr. Ryder does not make alone. This marriage depends not on the mutual consent of the couple but on the desire of the community to at once preserve its black origins and to attain the same social and economic status of whites.

Mr. Ryder chooses to marry Liza Jane, a woman who shares neither his aesthetic nor economic values, because his community's commitment to race, and ultimately his own, trumps both. It is only after the community recommends that "he should acknowledge her" that Mr. Ryder reveals the truth of his origins by introducing the wife of his youth.[74] That his past, represented by the figure of Liza Jane, should contrast so sharply with his present circumstances seems to suggest the possibility of leaving relations formed in slavery behind. But there is also a certain poignancy to Liza Jane's commitment, her unwavering desire to be reunited with the man slavery had separated her from, that manifests the flaws of the Blue Veins' program for racial uplift. The advances the Blue Veins seem to have achieved rely on their belief that their light-colored skin entitles them to certain advantages that are denied those with darker skin. Their deep investment in skin color implicates the Blue Veins in continuing the racial logic of slavery, even though they are more than a generation removed from it. It is no wonder then that the slave-marriage, while lacking legal sanction, is deemed to be the proper one, as it is based not on the rational and distinctly modern forces of economic and social advancement but on an outmoded commitment to a racial past that used blood and skin to determine the economic prospects and social position of the individual. The symbolic power of marriage, even for this community committed to middle-class values, lies primarily in continuing the racial logic that deems blacks inferior to whites.

"Exercising the civil right to marry," as Claudia Tate writes in her influential account of turn-of-the-century black marriage plots, "was as important to the newly freed black population as exercising another civil right . . . Negro suffrage."[75] However, in "The Wife of His Youth," the parallel Tate draws between marriage and a former slave's "rights" is presented as an obstacle to both individual freedom and social progress. Legalizing bonds formed in slavery by performing marriages in Reconstruction defeats its purpose. Such marriages, as Uncle Wellington and Mr. Ryder manifest, defy the progressive movement of the marriage plot. In the end, Mr. Ryder is willing to give up the material benefits promised by a marriage to Molly Dixon in order to honor a promise made in slavery. Ultimately, Mr. Ryder's identity is determined not by his present circumstances but by the racial logic of slavery that binds him to Liza Jane.

By figuring Mr. Ryder's racial commitment in the form of a marriage plot, Chesnutt transforms race into a moral issue that he develops in a subsequent story in the collection, regarding yet another "prominent member" of the Blue Veins. In "A Matter of Principle," Chesnutt introduces Cicero Clayton, whose "fundamental . . . social creed was that he himself was not a negro."[76] Like Mr. Ryder's desire for social advancement and respectability, Clayton's creed is similarly committed to overcoming what Nancy Bentley calls the "stigma" of race through marriage. However, unlike Mr. Ryder who is so focused on his own marital prospects, Clayton looks to the marriage of his only daughter, "the queen of her social set," to comply with the dictates of his "social creed."[77] Significantly, Clayton passes on his "principles" (what Chesnutt equates in the story with the logic of racial inheritance) to his daughter by arranging her marriage. But so obsessed are the Claytons with proving themselves not to be "negro" that the pleasures and privileges of marriage are ultimately denied them:

> Among Miss Clayton's friends and associates matrimony took on an added seriousness because of the very narrow limits within which it could take place. Miss Clayton and her friends, by reason of their assumed superiority to black people, or perhaps as much by reason of a somewhat morbid shrinking from the curiosity manifested toward married people of strongly contrasting colors, would not marry black men, and except in rare instances white men would not marry them. They were therefore restricted for a choice to the young men of their own complexion.[78]

The link between race and marriage makes marriage "a serious matter," for it is not only the pleasures and desires of the couple that are at stake. Of equal importance to the intimacy marriage represents is "a higher conception of the brotherhood of man."[79] However, Clayton's rhetoric against race proves false when he tries, but fails, to arrange Alice's marriage by attending closely to the racial qualities of her suitor at the expense of his other qualities. While Alice's marriage is key to establishing her social status as "not a negro," the meticulous attention she must pay to racial qualifications to secure her "superior" social position "leaves her the innocent victim of circumstances and principles."[80] In the end, Alice's opportunity to marry an up-and-coming black congressman are ruined by her father's efforts to ensure that he is a suitable match for his daughter by making sure that he too is "not a negro." The importance Clayton places on discerning racial difference, an importance he euphemistically calls "a matter of principle," leads Alice into the arms of her "last chance," Jack, a man who offers her little social or economic advancement but "was as fair of complexion as she."[81]

It is precisely this obsession with race on the part of those who claim to want nothing to do with it that interferes with the love story that conventionally culminates in marriage. "Her Virginia Mammy" introduces Clara Hohlfelder, the adopted daughter of German immigrants, who withholds her response to a marriage proposal until she can determine her racial origins. Clara reasons that marrying without such knowledge has the potential to cause future harm to her lover. John, her beloved, remains unconvinced by Clara's "tragic view of life."[82] John wants to marry Clara because she is "[t]he best and sweetest woman on earth, who[m] [he] love[s] unspeakably."[83] Nevertheless, John's reason does not satisfy Clara. She counters his declaration of love with "the consciousness that [her origins were] not true would be always with me, poisoning my mind, and darkening my life and yours."[84] Clara fears that her origins would make her an unsuitable match for a doctor whose lineage makes him something of an American aristocrat. Although Clara remains ignorant of her past, it still has the power to "darken" her present and future. Chesnutt's play on words suggests that the investment in origins, whether they are known or unknown, is tied to racial thinking, a way of thinking that is linked here to Clara's "tragic view of life." In Chesnutt's *Stories of the Color Line*, the commitment to race turns the familiar happy ending of the marriage plot into the stuff of tragedy.

Clara's resistance to marrying John is initially presented as a side effect of her sentimental nature, while John's desire to marry her is deemed rational and right. Their different natures are reflected not only by their gender difference but also by their chosen professions. Clara's profession as a dance instructor demands sentimental creative expression, while John's medical career relies on scientific reason and rational judgment. Yet it is John who insists on marrying for love while Clara relies on common blood and ancestry before making her marital decision. Ironically, John's commitment to love is backed by science and reason. "For the past we can claim no credit," John explains to Clara, "for those who made it die with it. Our destiny lies in the future."[85] Clara cannot refute John's logic. Instead, she merely sighs and agrees. "I know all that. But I am not like you. A woman is not like a man; she cannot lose herself in theories and generalizations."[86] However, Clara is more committed to "theories and generalizations" than her status as a woman might suggest. Her idea of marriage has less to do with what she feels than with her belief in racial ancestry. Where we come from, for Clara, determines not only who we are but also who should marry whom.

Nonetheless, the sacrifice Mr. Ryder makes in "The Wife of His Youth" to preserve his honor and racial commitments are overturned by the story of "Her Virginia Mammy." This time it is Clara who relates her story to a former slave, Mrs. Harper, who, unknown to her, happens to be her very own mother who sacrificed her daughter in order to protect her from the bonds of slavery. Clara's story reveals a connection and resemblance between the two women: "As they stood for a moment, the mirror reflecting and framing their image, more than one point of resemblance between them was emphasized."[87] Clara misses not only the resemblance but other, even more obvious, signs of Mrs. Harper's maternity. "Mrs. Harper, following her movements with a suppressed intensity of interest which Clara, had she not been absorbed in her own thoughts, could not have failed to observe."[88] Mrs. Harper recounts the circumstances of Clara's birth but leaves out the fact that she, who had once been a slave, is her mother. Clara's happiness rests significantly on "the strong effort with which Mrs. Harper controlled herself" from revealing their connection; by doing so, Mrs. Harper allows Clara to believe that she is the legitimate daughter of a "Virginia gentleman," and so the social equal of the man she hopes to marry.[89] In this case, *not* acknowledging the intimacy of a past relation leads to the protagonist's happiness. In the end, whatever Clara believes to be the truth of her origins and social status amounts to very little since, as John informs her, she will have to forsake her past once they are married. The marital union between this daughter of a former slave and the great-grandson of the governor of Connecticut has the potential to eliminate the differences between them.[90] With her newfound knowledge of her origins, Clara accepts not only John's marriage proposal but also his theory that "our destiny lies in the future."[91]

Although Clara does find happiness by leaving her slave mother behind, Chesnutt goes on to show that the self-control Mrs. Harper exhibits to enable her daughter's happiness is the exception that proves the rule of race. "Cicely's Dream," more than any other story in *The Wife of His Youth and Other Stories of the Color Line*, comes closest to being a full-fledged love story. Not surprisingly, it ends tragically. Unlike the collection's other stories in which love seems incidental to the terms of a good marriage, "Cicely's Dream" presents love as being essential to it. The story (up until the final devastating paragraph) is told entirely from Cicely's perspective and recounts the circumstances that lead her to fall in love with an unknown soldier she discovers wounded in the bushes.

It all starts with a dream in which "she had first tasted the sweetness of love."[92] Cicely is able to realize her dream because the man she loves, by a happy coincidence, has no memory of his past. Without any barriers to their union, Cicely and the man whom she calls "John" fall in love and plan to marry. However, Cicely's happiness is abruptly interrupted when her fiancé regains his memory upon meeting "the wife of his youth." However, this wife is not a former slave but a white schoolteacher from the North who moves South "in the sublime and not unfruitful effort to transform three millions of slaves into intelligent freemen" when her beloved does not return from the war. The reunion between the northern lovers leaves Cicely, and the project of freedom and Reconstruction for that matter, forgotten. Like the dream that opens the story, Cicely's love story is just as suddenly "dashed from her lips, and she could not even enjoy the memory of it, except in a vague, indefinite, and tantalizing way."[93]

Cicely does not face the racial dilemma Mr. Ryder confronts when he meets again the wife of his youth since she understands from the outset that love is determined by race. Cicely knows very little of love; the little she does know comes from a dream. "[O]nly in her dream had she known or thought of love as something supremely desirable."[94] And love remains only a dream at the end of the story because it is race and not love or Cicely's desire to realize her dream that ultimately determines the marriage with which the story concludes. Despite Cicely's ignorance of its social and legal conventions, she is supremely aware that race plays an essential role in determining whom she can or cannot love. "If the wounded man were of her own race, her dream would thus far have been realized, and having met the young man the other joys might be expected to follow. If he should turn out to be a white man, then her dream was clearly one of the kind that go by contraries, and she could expect only sorrow and trouble and pains as the proper sequences of this fateful discovery."[95] In her interpretation of her dream, Cicely takes for granted the fact that her happiness depends upon the race of the man she loves. The point of the story, however, is found in the fact that she cannot discern his race and does not learn it until she has fallen in love with him—at which moment race answers the question of whether or not their love will culminate in marriage. Race prevents a happy ending. When her lover regains his memory, Cicely loses not only the man she loves but also "the golden key to the avenues of opportunity" that would have been hers had she married the man of her dream.

□ □ □

Chesnutt's *The Wife of His Youth and Other Stories of the Color Line* is set against the historical circumstances regarding marriage practices among the newly freed black population. The circumstances are framed by the "blended" emotions of Chesnutt's characters, who struggle to find love and happiness within the constraints of racial classification. When placed in such a fictional context, the equality promised by marriage replaces the literal bonds of slavery with a figural double bind. Marriage, as Chesnutt presents it, promises freedom, but the promise can only be kept by making an unequivocal break with the past. Few make it. Some, like Olivia Cartaret in the novel *The Marrow of Tradition*, are unable; others, like Mr. Ryder in "The Wife of His Youth," are unwilling. While Chesnutt's *The Wife of His Youth and Other Stories of the Color Line* designates the Civil War as the beginning of the end of slavery, the war, as these stories imply, can only end the practice of slavery, not the relationships formed by it. The bonds between master and slave reemerge in the form of voluntary marital bonds between slaves that were affirmed after the war. The legalization of slave-marriages after the war encouraged the newly freed to preserve relationships formed in slavery, making marriage at least as much a matter of racial affiliation as it was of personal choice—or, to put it more plainly, of love. Why did the absence of marriage during slavery make it so important to the articulation of freedom? Was marriage essential to Reconstruction or was it responsible for its failure? These questions, which reemerge with every serious attempt to grapple with the realities of Jim Crow segregation, preoccupied Chesnutt more than has been acknowledged.[96] Perhaps, Chesnutt leads readers to wonder, tying marriage so strongly to the idea of freedom and race in the post-emancipation era has made it impossible for free black Americans to marry for love.

In a letter to his publishers, Houghton, Mifflin & Co., confirming publication of his collection, Chesnutt reflects upon its title, a title that he admits to have been selected for him by his editor but that was appropriate nonetheless because "all the stories deal with that subject directly." Chesnutt goes on to explain that unlike his earlier collection of stories, *The Conjure Woman*, this one does not depend upon a character like Uncle Julius, "but a subject, as indicated in the title—the Color Line."[97] Published just a year before W. E. B. Du Bois would famously declare that "[t]he problem of the twentieth century is the problem of the color line," Chesnutt's *Stories of the Color Line* understands the color line not as a set of legal or economic conditions but as a series of subjects—Mr. Ryder, Cicero Clayton, Clara Hohlfelder, and Cicely—all of whom subscribe to the racial sentiments that once made slavery a reality. Du Bois, as is well known, reiterated his commitment to dismantling the color line by uncovering ideological, social, and economic barriers put in place by white Americans to inhibit the advancement of those whom Du Bois calls "black folk." As contemporaries, Chesnutt and Du Bois shared a personal and intellectual commitment to addressing the problem of the color line. While critics have been quick to discuss the similarities between these two "black intellectuals," they have been less forthcoming in examining the ways in which Chesnutt's stories depart from the Du Boisian view of culture.[98]

In Chesnutt's *Stories of the Color Line*, we are introduced to black characters struggling not with the legal or external barriers of racial classifications and proscriptions but instead with private attitudes toward love and marriage. The insecurity of living with one another without legal sanction made marriage a priority for the newly freed. However, the domestic security promised by a legal marriage, as Chesnutt's fiction illustrates, was circumscribed by attachments formed by slavery. While Chesnutt, like Du Bois after him, was committed to lifting the veil of race from American political and social life, his stories present the color line as the consequence of a personal commitment to preserving the racial logic of slavery. Without a promise made in slavery, Mr. Ryder is free to marry Molly Dixon and continue his pursuit of wealth and social status—but by doing so he would also betray the woman who enabled the middle-class pursuits he now enjoys. Through the dramatization of such dual commitments in his fiction, Chesnutt's *The Wife of His Youth and Other Stories of the Color Line* makes the idea of the slave-marriage central to the discourse of race in the post-emancipation United States.

Conclusion

Reading Hannah Crafts
in the Twenty-First Century

The uneasy connection between race and marriage Chesnutt develops in his fiction is drawn, as I argue in chapter 5, upon his attempt to grapple with the intimate dimension of the history of slavery. Writing well after the end of legal slavery in the United States, Chesnutt remains fascinated and troubled by its lingering social effects during his lifetime. Whether to erase slavery's effects or preserve them for the sake of posterity and community was a problem that Chesnutt, at least in his published works, could not resolve. Coming to terms with the logic of the slave-marriage and its peculiar nonlegal status does not, as Chesnutt shows in his fiction, disappear with the Emancipation Proclamation, nor does it end, as Toni Morrison, Sherley Anne Williams, Edward P. Jones, and a number of writers of later slave fictions insist, with the passage of legislation legalizing unions between previously nonlegal and illegal unions.

Writing about slave-marriages in the late-twentieth century, Morrison's Nobel Prize–winning fiction exemplifies the possibility of imagining a form of racial intimacy that transcends the law. As we see in the case of her novel *Beloved*, such intimacy has a destructive potential that needs somehow to be checked by those who are held by its power. Unlike Morrison's and other more recent critically acclaimed slave fictions, the ones I examine in this book were written in a context in which the importance of legal marriage to the constitution of freedom was largely taken for granted. Slave law mandated marriage as a contract into which slaves could not legally enter. By calling into question this legal fact, these fictions offer us a way of thinking and writing about marriage outside of legal discourse.

To conclude, then, I would like to turn to a new, yet old, slave fiction: Hannah Crafts's *The Bondwoman's Narrative*. The first edition of *The Bondwoman's Narrative* was published in the spring of 2002. According to its editor, Henry Louis Gates, the novel was written by a female fugitive slave in the 1850s, though it was never published during the author's lifetime. The book's gripping, visceral depictions of slave life and an escape to the North are familiar to readers of the slave narratives. It is no wonder that Gates—among others—elides the autobiographical and fictional elements of the text. Calling it "an autobiographical novel written between 1853 and 1860," Gates and his co-editor, Hollis Robbins, encourage readers to read the work as "historical fact." Gates and Robbins build "a strong case" through their research "that she is who she says she is—that she is female, that she is of African descent, that she is a slave who grew up in Virginia."[1] Yet not everyone is convinced that Crafts is who she says she is. While admitting to being "*almost* persuaded," Eric Gardner contends that "we do not definitively know who Hannah Crafts was."[2] The stakes of not knowing the facts of Crafts's biography are higher than one might expect. Without these facts, Gardner states, we cannot "fully place her within African American letters." What, then, are we to do with Hannah Crafts's *The Bondwoman's Narrative*?

To conclude, I would like to return to the tension between history and fiction that I raised in the introduction. By doing so, I read Crafts's novel not as historical fact but as a slave fiction, a form that presents experience through the eyes of a slave. This perspective, fictional though it may be, offers readers today insights into the past that was not, for various reasons, contained by historical accounts of slavery.

Although they arrive at very different conclusions about Crafts's novel, both Gates and Gardner are troubled by how to understand and classify the fictional elements of Crafts's slave story in relation to its depiction of slavery. Crafts's novel is told from the singular perspective of a female slave. But because this narrative is explicitly fiction, as several of its recent readers note, it does not participate in the abolitionist discourse of nineteenth-century political thought. So, what is the point of this singular slave fiction, and why read it in the twenty-first century when it had no impact at the time it was first written in the mid-nineteenth century? As I have been suggesting through readings of nineteenth-century slave fictions, part of the interest in these novels today lies in their depictions of marriage. Echoing almost verbatim the sentiments of her fellow slave-novelist William Wells Brown, the slave's escape is precipitated by her mistress's efforts "to force me into a compulsory union with a man whom I could only hate and despise."[3] Prior to this event, our narrator exhibits a good deal of forbearance, even though she is opposed to slavery: "Marriage like many other blessings I considered to be especially designed for the free, and something that all the victims of slavery should avoid as tending essentially to perpetuate that system." It is not clear if Crafts here, as elsewhere, is attacking the institution of slavery or marriage. It is, of course, the combination between the two that is particularly irksome to her. Although she views a slave-marriage with only "loathing and disgust," she realizes that it offers the best way to live happily as a slave. Like Brown, who outsmarts Mrs. Price, Crafts's narrator avoids the marriage trap set for her by Mrs. Wheeler by feigning submission. In the end, Hannah manages to overcome tremendous odds and escapes from slavery to enjoy "the undeviating happiness . . . in the society of my mother, my husband and my friends." Concluding with this image of a happy marriage that looks forward to Harper's 1892 novel, *Iola Leroy*, Crafts, with some irony, writes: "I will let the reader picture it all to his imagination and say farewell."[4] The happy marriage with which the author concludes is fictional—something to be imagined rather than experienced—and it is a marriage between a former slave and a man who "has always been a free man." Crafts thus escapes from slavery to avoid a marriage and enters into a marriage upon acquiring her freedom. Of course, the marriage she escapes and the marriage we picture at the end of the novel are two very different kinds of marriages. But the image of the free marriage with which Crafts concludes her novel exists side by side with a slave-marriage, a marriage formed between two slaves with the consent of both their masters. Unlike the one Mrs. Wheeler proposes for Hannah, the slave-marriage Hannah witnesses is a loving and consensual one, though still nonlegal.

Recovering from injuries sustained by her attempt to outwit the villainous lawyer, appropriately called Mr. Trappe, Hannah finds herself in the home of a benevolent white couple. It is here where she witnesses the slave-marriage between Charlotte and William. Hannah provides a detailed description of the event, since it marks also her recovery and reentry into the world of slavery she had attempted to leave behind. Carefully recording the minute details of the wedding ceremony, this is one of the happier moments in a novel that is generally preoccupied by "acts of cruelty" that "fill the soul with the deepest horror."[5] The slave wedding Crafts witnesses marks a radical shift in her experience of slavery.

> How well I remember the pleasant evening when I left my room for the first time to enjoy the social conviviality of a wedding party. Mrs. Henry who seemed

sent into the world to dispense good-feeling and Happiness loved to indulge her servants in all innocent pleasures not inconsistent with their duties. Her favorite slave, a beautiful Quadroon was to be married that night to a young man belonging to a neighboring estate, and the amiable mistress determined to make the nuptials of one the occasion of a holiday for the whole establishment.[6]

Hannah goes on to describe the attire of not just the bride and bridegroom but also that of the other slaves in attendance and the joyous reception that follows the ceremony. Hannah watches and witnesses these scenes from a distance, although she is still very much involved in the "great state of mirthful enjoyment" the event produces. It is only when the wedding party has dispersed that Hannah returns to her characteristic "dreary" and "gloomy" voice.

> I gazed at them and wondered if they were really so happy—wondered if no dark shadows of coming evil never haunted their minds. Then I thought of the young couple, who had so recently taken the vows and incurred the responsibilities of marriage—vows and responsibilities strangely fearful when taken in connection with their servile condition. Did the future spread before them bright and cloudless? Did they anticipate domestic felicity, and long years of wedded love: when their lives, their limbs, their very souls were subject to the control of another's will; when the husband could not be at liberty to provide a home for his wife, nor the wife be permitted to attend to the wants of her husband, and when living apart in a state of separate bondage they could only meet occasionally at best, and then might be decreed without a moment's warning to never meet again.[7]

Here Hannah struggles to gain perspective on the happy wedding she witnesses. Although the wedding scene is happy, Hannah has to remind herself, and her readers, that this marriage is not what it appears to be. It may look like a happy marriage, but as a slave-marriage it *cannot* be happy. The irony behind Hannah's critique of the slave-marriage is that Charlotte and William, against the narrator's persuasive arguments deriding the practice of slave-marriage, actually do enjoy the domestic felicity and long years of wedded love that Hannah believes will elude them because they are slaves. Charlotte and William eventually successfully escape from slavery together and the reason they escape, like the fictional George and Eliza Harris and the historical William and Ellen Craft, is to stay together. William puts the matter bluntly to Hannah when she discovers him to be the "ghost" believed by the other slaves to be haunting the place: "Our minds are fixed; they cannot be changed, because we have no alternative. We must either be separated or run away, and which, think you, that an affectionate wife should choose?"[8] In other words, William and Charlotte would rather die than be separated.

By choosing marriage over life, we understand the commitment between Charlotte and William to surpass the limits of legal marriage. William goes on to explain that if he wasn't married to Charlotte, he would not think of running away. Moreover, it is precisely *because* he is married that his master decides to sell him. "My master sold me to a southern trader, through sheer cruelty, I believe, and because he said that I was proud of my marriage."[9] The owner is driven by his desire to destroy marriage while the slave is driven by his desire to protect it.

But Hannah is not driven by such a desire. Hannah refuses to join Charlotte and William on their quest for freedom. As she explains to them, she has to protect herself and this means remaining a slave. It is the slave couple's successful escape that reveals to both Hannah and Charlotte's mistress, Mrs. Henry, the true meaning of marriage. Charlotte's marriage and escape are against the law, but her actions are deemed—in the eyes of God and her mistress—to be right. "'And yet I cannot find it in my heart to blame her,' remarked the amiable woman. 'I ought to have foreseen all this, and yet I did not. The language of Scripture is just as true to-day as it was six thousand years ago. "Thy desire shall be thy husband." For him Charlotte could abandon her home, and long-tried friends. Heaven grant, that he prove worthy of the trust, and that they may reach in safety the land of freedom.'"[10] When Charlotte and William reappear at the end of the story, they have indeed reached the land of freedom. Having lost track of them after their escape, the couple miraculously reappears in New Jersey where they turn out to be Hannah's neighbors. These former slaves now occupy a kind of paradise in New Jersey, reminiscent of *Dred*'s Lisette and Harry's southern home: "a tiny white cottage half-shaded in summer by rose-vines and honeysuckle appears at the foot of a sloping green. In front there is such an exquisite flower-garden, and behind such a dainty orchard of choice fruits that it does one good to think of it."[11] There is ultimately no difference between the free marriage she imagines for herself and the slave-marriage between Charlotte and William. Marriage is, ultimately, a figment of the author's imagination in both cases. The key to both is to escape the trap of falling into a bad marriage like that of Hannah's mistress on the Lindendale plantation, a trap that is embodied by an unscrupulous lawyer. Set against one another by the relationship they share with Hannah's mistress, Mr. Trappe and Hannah embody opposing philosophies of marriage. Involved in an intricate plan of bribery and extortion, Mr. Trappe views marriage as a means by which he might accumulate capital and thereby improve his social standing. Hannah, on the other hand, stands for love and fidelity and is willing to risk her life to protect her mistress from complying with the dictates of Mr. Trappe's law. Although all lawyers are not as helpfully called Mr. Trappe, some are called Mr. Stevens, as in Webb's *The Garies and Their Friends*, and some go by the ironic name of Mr. Wright, as in Chesnutt's "Uncle Wellington's Wives." Whatever they are called, legal figures in these stories of slavery turn out to have the wrong ideas about marriage. Slaves, who are outside the law, exhibit a surprising knowledge of the rights and wrongs of marriage.

Discerning between the right and wrong kinds of marriages constitutes the work of slave fiction; in the process of showing us marriage not protected or bound by law, these fictions inevitably tell a story of marriage that relies on slavery. We read *The Bondwoman's Narrative* today not because it was written by a female slave of African descent, although it may have been. We read it for the intimate history of slavery that Crafts records. In reading her novel and other nineteenth-century slave fictions, I hope to have offered a way to broaden our understanding of the history of marriage from the legal discourse to which it has, and continues to be, bound.

Notes

Introduction: The Slave-Marriage Plot

1. Bibb, Henry, *Narrative of the Life and Adventures of Henry Bibb, an American Slave, Written by Himself.* 1849; repr., Madison: University of Wisconsin Press, 2001.

2. George L. Christian and Frank W. Christian, "Slave-Marriages," *Virginia Law Journal* 1, no. 11 (November 1877): 644.

3. William Andrews, *To Tell a Free Story: The First Century of Afro-American Autobiography, 1760–1855* (Urbana: University of Illinois Press, 1988), 144–45.

4. William Wells Brown, *Clotel; or, The President's Daughter* (1853; repr., Boston: Bedford/St. Martin's, 2000), 84. All further quotations from *Clotel* will be from this edition.

5. Brown, *Clotel,* 83.

6. I use the term "higher law" in this context to distinguish the slave-marriage as a union formulated on moral grounds. While there are a number of different and often conflicting definitions of the term, it can be summed up as drawing upon a moral understanding of laws that look to a heavenly authority for ratification. For a full discussion of the term and its use during the period in which Brown writes, see Gregg D. Crane, *Race, Citizenship, and Law in American Literature* (New York: Cambridge University Press, 2002), 1–55.

7. I borrow this phrase from Jane Tompkins, who uses it to great effect in her influential account of the political import of nineteenth-century domestic fiction with particular emphasis on Harriet Beecher Stowe's *Uncle Tom's Cabin;* Jane Tompkins, *Sentimental Designs: The Cultural Work of American Fiction, 1790–1860* (New York: Oxford University Press, 1985), 125. I use the term in relation to Brown, however, to mark the difference between his fictional and nonfictional accounts of slave-marriage. In his autobiography, *Narrative of William W. Brown, a Fugitive Slave,* published six years before the first edition of *Clotel* appeared, Brown presents a less-sentimental picture of slave-marriages. Based upon his personal experience, Brown explains that slaveholders used marriages between slaves as a fairly effective method of dissuading slaves from running away. Unlike the "many slaves" who did marry, Brown, he tells us, had the good sense to wait until after his escape from slavery. Chapter 1 discusses the differences between Brown's fictional and nonfictional

representations of slave-marriage by drawing upon the particular, and highly unusual, circumstances of Brown's own marital experiences.

8. I borrow this phrase from Sutton E. Griggs, who uses it as the title of the thirteenth and fourteenth chapters of his novel, *Imperium in Imperio* (1899).

9. John Locke's *Subjection of Women* (1861) and Mary Wollstonecraft's *A Vindication of the Rights of Women* (1792) provide early and particularly persuasive accounts of the connection between slavery, marriage, and freedom. Needless to say, their ideas about slavery differ significantly from the writers who are the subject of this study.

10. Hendrik Hartog, *Man and Wife in America* (Cambridge, Mass.: Harvard University Press, 2000), 2. Although the term "contract" does operate both literally and metaphorically in the nineteenth century, the slave-marriage is defined by its place outside contractual relations. While legal and literary historians are quick to equate contract with freedom, the slave-marriage suggests the capacity for marital relations to be formed without or despite its refusal to recognize slaves. We might therefore think of the slave-marriage both symbolically and literally, an instance in which slaves act against the law without acquiring freedom of contract. On the metaphorical resonances of contract as a symbol of freedom during the post-emancipation period, see Amy Dru Stanley, *From Bondage to Contract: Wage Labor, Marriage, and the Market in the Age of Slave Emancipation* (Cambridge: Cambridge University Press, 1998), x.

11. Drucilla Cornell, *The Imaginary Domain* (New York: Routledge, 1988).

12. Frances Smith Foster's recent editorial and critical scholarship on *Love and Marriage in Early African America* is a significant exception to this rule. See *'Til Death or Distance Do Us Part: Love and Marriage in African America* (New York: Oxford University Press, 2010) and *Love and Marriage in Early African America* (Boston: Northeastern University Press, 2007).

13. Emily West, *Chains of Love: Slave Couples in Antebellum South Carolina* (Urbana: University of Illinois Press, 2004), 20.

14. Histories of slave culture experienced something of a boom in the mid-1970s with the publication of Daniel Patrick Moynihan's infamous "Report on the Black Family." The list of histories I provide here represents some of the most influential accounts of slave-marriages in the nineteenth century. For instance, John Blassingame, *The Slave Community: Plantation Life in the Antebellum South* (Oxford: Oxford University Press, 1979); Herbert G. Gutman, *The Black Family in Slavery and Freedom, 1750–1925* (New York: Pantheon Books, 1976); Eugene D. Genovese, *Roll, Jordan, Roll: The World the Slaves Made* (New York: Pantheon Books, 1974); Elizabeth Fox-Genovese, *Within the Plantation Household: Black and White Women of the Old South* (Chapel Hill: University of North Carolina Press, 1988); Charles Joyner, *Down by the Riverside: A South Carolina Slave Community* (Urbana: University of Illinois Press, 1984); Deborah Gray White, *Ar'n't I a Woman: Female Slaves in the Plantation South* (New York: W. W. Norton, 1999).

15. Martha Hodes, *White Women, Black Men: Illicit Sex in the Nineteenth-Century South* (New Haven, Conn.: Yale University Press, 1997), 1.

16. Frederick Douglass, *My Bondage and My Freedom* (New York: Miller, Orton & Mulligan, 1855).

17. Ashraf Rushdy, *Neo-Slave Narratives: Studies in the Social Logic of a Literary Form* (New York: Oxford University Press, 1999).

18. Hodes, *White Women, Black Men,* 1.

19. John Ernest, *Liberation Historiography: African American Writers and the Challenge of History, 1794–1861* (Chapel Hill: University of North Carolina Press, 2004), 6.

20. Ernest, *Liberation Historiography,* 7.

21. Ernest, *Liberation Historiography,* 9.

22. Lee Holcombe's book on married women's property remains the most complete account of these debates; Lee Holcombe, *Wives and Property: Reform of the Married Women's Property Law in Nineteenth-Century England* (Toronto: University of Toronto Press, 1983). For an account of the debate over coverture in nineteenth-century America and the problematic parallel drawn between wives and slaves, see Nancy Cott, *Public Vows: A History of Marriage and the Nation* (Cambridge, Mass.: Harvard University Press, 2002), 64–71. Also see Hartog, *Man and Wife in America,* 115–35.

23. See Lydia Maria Child, *The History of the Condition of Women, in Various Ages and Nations* (New York, 1835); Sarah Grimké, *Letters on the Equality of the Sexes and the Condition of Women* (Boston, 1838).

24. Lydia Maria Child, "Slavery's Pleasant Homes" and Other Writings from the Liberty Bell. Online Archive of Nineteenth-Century U.S. Women's Writings, ed. Glynis Carr, originally published 1843, http://www.facstaff.bucknell.edu/gcarr/19cusww/LB/ (accessed December 6, 2010).

25. Carolyn L. Karcher, "Rape, Murder and Revenge in 'Slavery's Pleasant Homes': Lydia Maria Child's Antislavery Fiction and the Limits of Genre," *Women's Studies International Forum* 9, no. 4 (1986): 324.

26. Child, "Slavery's Pleasant Homes," paragraph 1.

27. Child, "Slavery's Pleasant Homes."

28. Harriet Jacobs, *Incidents in the Life of a Slave Girl, Written by Herself,* edited by Lydia Maria Child (Boston: Published for the Author, 1861), 58.

29. Jacobs, *Incidents in the Life of a Slave Girl,* 302.

30. In her discussion of *Clotel,* duCille describes the new fictive world Brown creates as "an 'unreal estate,' a fictive realm of the fantastic and coincidental . . . an ideologically charged space, created by drawing together a variety of discursive fields—including 'the real' and 'the romantic,' the simple and the sensational, the allegorical and the historical." Ann duCille, *The Coupling Convention: Sex, Text, and Tradition in Black Women's Fiction* (New York: Oxford University Press, 1993), 18.

31. Blassingame, *The Slave Community.*

32. Harriet Beecher Stowe, *Uncle Tom's Cabin* (1852; repr., New York: Norton, 1999), 14.

33. Stowe, *Uncle Tom's Cabin,* 15.

34. Lydia Maria Child, *The Freedmen's Book* (Boston: Ticknor and Fields, 1865), 193.

35. Ann duCille outlines much of the critical controversy surrounding Brown's novel and its connection to DNA tests performed in the late 1990s that "established a strong probability that Jefferson fathered at least one of Sally Hemings's children." See Ann duCille, "Where in the World Is William Wells Brown? Thomas Jefferson, Sally Hemings, and the DNA of African-American Literary History," *American Literary History* 12, no. 3 (2000): 446.

36. Claudia Tate, *Domestic Allegories of Political Desire: The Black Heroine's Text at the Turn of the Century* (New York: Oxford University Press, 1992), 8–9.

37. Katherine Franke, "Becoming a Citizen: Post-Bellum Regulation of African American Marriage," *Yale Journal of Law and the Humanities* 11 (1999): 252.

38. Charles W. Chesnutt, *Stories, Novels and Essays* (New York: Library Classics of the United States, 2002), 213.

Chapter 1: Between Fiction and Experience

1. See William Wells Brown, *Narrative of William W. Brown, a Fugitive Slave, Written by Himself* (London: Charles Gilpin, 1849). Hereafter cited by page number as *Narrative*.

2. *Narrative*, v.

3. Frederick Douglass, *My Bondage and My Freedom* (New York: Miller, Orton, and Mulligan, 1855), 409.

4. William Wells Brown, *Clotel; or, The President's Daughter: A Narrative of Slave Life in the United States* (1853; repr. Boston: Bedford/St. Martin's, 2000), 83. Hereafter cited by page number as *Clotel*.

5. John Blassingame, *The Slave Community: Plantation Life in the Antebellum South* (Oxford: Oxford University Press, 1979); Herbert G. Gutman, *The Black Family in Slavery and Freedom, 1750–1925* (New York: Pantheon Books, 1976); Eugene D. Genovese, *Roll, Jordan, Roll: The World the Slaves Made* (New York: Pantheon Books, 1974); Elizabeth Fox-Genovese, *Within the Plantation Household: Black and White Women of the Old South* (Chapel Hill: University of North Carolina Press, 1988); Charles Joyner, *Down by the Riverside: A South Carolina Slave Community* (Urbana: University of Illinois Press, 1984); Deborah Gray White, *Ar'n't I a Woman: Female Slaves in the Plantation South* (New York: W. W. Norton, 1999). For a recent and engaging literary history of slave (and free) marriages, see Frances Smith Foster, *'Til Death or Distance Do Us Part: Love and Marriage in African America* (New York: Oxford University Press, 2010).

6. *Narrative*, 84.

7. *Narrative*, 85.

8. *Narrative*, 90.

9. Focusing on Brown's historical writings, Russ Castronovo argues, "These diverse autobiographical accounts do not so much constitute a complete life, inviolable in the authority of its own experiences, as they subtly reconstitute history, implying its mutable and selective aspects." See Russ Castronovo, *Fathering the Nation: American Genealogies of Slavery and Freedom* (Berkeley: University of California Press, 1995), 67.

10. See William Wells Brown, "Narrative of the Life and Escape of William Wells Brown," in *Clotel*. See also William Wells Brown, *Memoir of William Wells Brown, an American Bondman, Written by Himself* (Boston: Boston Anti-Slavery Office, 1859) and *My Southern Home; or, the South and Its People* (Boston: H. G. Brown, 1880).

11. For a different reading of Brown's narration of literacy acquisition, see Stephen Lucasi, "William Wells Brown's Narrative & Traveling Subjectivity," *African American Review* 41, no. 3 (2007): 521–22, in which he links the mobility that literacy offers Brown to the form of his later travel narratives.

12. As James Hammerton explains in his illuminating study of divorce in the nineteenth century, marital discord mostly remained private and secluded from the public eye, except

when some sensational litigation or shaming communal ritual exposed private misconduct to wider scrutiny. See James Hammerton, *Cruelty and Companionship: Conflict in
Nineteenth-Century Married Life* (New York: Routledge, 1992), 1.

13. See William Andrews, *To Tell a Free Story: The First Century of Afro-American
Autobiography, 1760–1855* (Urbana: University of Illinois Press, 1988), 165.

14. *Narrative*, 24, 88.

15. See Ann duCille, *The Coupling Convention: Sex, Text, and Tradition in Black Women's
Fiction* (New York: Oxford University Press, 1993), 19.

16. *Clotel*, 82.

17. *Narrative*, 88.

18. "Public," in *William Wells Brown: A Reader*, ed. Ezra Greenspan (Athens: University
of Georgia Press, 2008), 447.

19. See Elizabeth S. Brown, "A Stray Husband," *New York Daily Tribune*, 12 March 1850.

20. "Public," 450.

21. Stephanie Coontz, *Marriage, a History: From Obedience to Intimacy or How Love
Conquered Marriage* (New York: Viking, 2005), 7.

22. See William Edward Farrison, *William Wells Brown: Author, Reformer* (Chicago:
University of Chicago Press, 1969), 62.

23. "Public," 449.

24. "Public," 450.

25. *Narrative*, 213.

26. Michael Warner, *Public and Counterpublics* (New York: Zone Books, 2002), 30.

27. "Public," 449.

28. William Wells Brown, "Narrative of William W. Brown, A Fugitive Slave," in *From
Fugitive Slave to Free Man: The Autobiographies of William Wells Brown*, ed. William
Andrews (Columbia: University of Missouri Press, 2003), 82.

29. See John Ernest, *Resistance and Reformation in Nineteenth-Century African-American Literature: Brown, Wilson, Jacobs, Delany, Douglass, and Harper* (Jackson: University
Press of Mississippi, 1998).

30. *Clotel*, 82.

31. *Clotel*, 83.

32. *Clotel*, 83.

33. *Clotel*, 83.

34. *Clotel*, 83.

35. *Narrative*, 213.

36. *Clotel*, 86.

37. *Clotel*, 86. See Monique Guillory, "Under One Roof: The Sins and Sanctity of the
New Orleans Quadroon Balls," in *Race Consciousness*, ed. Judith Jackson Fossett and
Jeffrey A. Tucker, 67–82 (New York: New York University Press, 1997).

38. Guillory, "Under One Roof," 70.

39. *Clotel*, 101–2.

40. *Clotel*, 102.

41. *Clotel*, 122.

42. *Clotel*, 101.

43. *Clotel*, 100.

44. Lydia Maria Child, "The Quadroons" (1842; repr. in Glynis Carr, ed., the Online Archive of Nineteenth-Century U.S. Women's Writings, summer 1997, http://www.facstaff .bucknell.edu/gcarr/19cUSWW/LB/Q.html (accessed December 6, 2010).

45. *Clotel*, 71.

46. *Clotel*, 120.

47. *Clotel*, 120.

48. *Clotel*, 121.

49. *Clotel*, 107.

50. *Clotel*, 107.

51. *Clotel*, 107.

52. *Clotel*, 108.

53. *Clotel*, 107.

54. *Clotel*, 108.

55. *Clotel*, 132.

56. *Clotel*, 143.

57. *Clotel*, 108.

58. *Clotel*, 108.

59. *Clotel*, 110.

60. *Clotel*, 159.

61. *Clotel*, 159.

62. *Clotel*, 160.

63. *Clotel*, 160.

64. Lucy Stone and her future husband, Henry B. Blackwell, were well known within the antislavery lecture circuit, where Brown may have encountered them. Their marriage in 1855 was something of a sensation in the period and was reported in several newspapers, including *Frederick Douglass' Paper*. Here, as elsewhere, the Stone–Blackwell marriage ceremony was reported as a protest against the laws of the commonwealth concerning marriage. See *Frederick Douglass' Paper*, May 11, 1855.

65. For Brown's account of the Crafts' escape from slavery, see his letter to William Lloyd Garrison, "The Flight of Ellen and William Craft," in *The Liberator*, January 12, 1849; repr. in Herbert Aptheker, ed., *A Documentary History of the Negro People in the United States* (New York: Citadel, 1969), 277–78.

66. *Clotel*, 225.

67. *Clotel*, 225.

68. *Clotel*, 225.

69. *Clotel*, 225.

70. *Clotel*, 225.

71. *Clotel*, 225.

72. William Wells Brown, *Clotelle, or, The Colored Heroine* (Boston: Lee and Shepard, 1867), 3.

Chapter 2: Dred *and the Freedom of Marriage*

1. Harriet Beecher Stowe, *Dred: A Tale of the Great Dismal Swamp*, ed. Robert S. Levine (New York: Penguin, 2000), 578. Hereafter cited by page number as *Dred*.

2. See Hendrik Hartog, *Man and Wife in America: A History* (Cambridge, Mass.: Harvard University Press, 2000), 93. See also George L. Christian and Frank W. Christian, "Slave-Marriages," in *Virginia Law Journal* 1, no. 11 (1877): 641–52, in which the authors consider the case of *Colson v. Quander* in which a free man of color in 1842 married a slave woman with the consent of her master. As one of the few legal cases in which a slave-marriage, "though void when made," was decided by the Special Court of Appeals to be legitimate "after the disability of slavery had ceased," this important case determined that "where slaves have permanently lived together as man and wife, and continue to live together as such after emancipation, the marriage is valid from the date of emancipation." In contrast to the legal history of slave-marriage, Stowe's novel considers the legitimacy of the slave-marriage *during*, rather than after, slavery.

3. Alexis de Tocqueville, *Democracy in America*, quoted in Herbert G. Gutman, *The Black Family in Slavery and Freedom, 1750–1925* (New York: Pantheon Books, 1976), xxi.

4. William Blackstone, *Commentaries on the Laws of England*, vol. 1 (Oxford: Clarendon Press, 1770), 442.

5. Sarah Grimké, "Marriage (1852–1857)," in *The Female Experience: An American Documentary*, ed. Gerda Lerner (New York: Oxford University Press, 1992), 95.

6. Harriet Beecher Stowe, *The Minister's Wooing* (1859; repr., London: Penguin, 1999), 72.

7. *Dred*, 32.

8. *Dred*, 27.

9. It is worth noting here that nowhere in either *Uncle Tom's Cabin* or *Dred* does Stowe equate slavery with marriage. In contrast to well-known women's rights activists like Elizabeth Cady Stanton and Victoria Woodhull who drew an analogy between antebellum slavery and marriage, Stowe viewed the abolition of slavery as essential to the reform of nineteenth-century marriage laws. Harriet Beecher Stowe, *Uncle Tom's Cabin* (1852; repr., New York: Norton, 1999).

10. Elizabeth Cady Stanton et al., *History of Woman Suffrage*, vol. 1, 1848–1861; vol. 2, 1861–1866 (1881; repr., Salem, N.H.: Ayer, 1985), 14–15.

11. It is worth noting that in the late 1860s, Stowe did make the connection between women and slaves more explicit in her nonfictional writings. For instance, in her article "The Woman Question," which appeared in the pages of *Hearth and Home* in 1868, Stowe shows how "the position of a married woman, under English common law, is, in many respects, precisely similar to that of the negro slave." To avoid further confusion concerning the connection, she goes on to explain that the law of marriage condones domestic violence just as slave law had condoned the use of violence in maintaining "the submission of the slave perfect."

12. The metaphoric linking of women and slaves has been the topic of considerable discussion and debate. While Stowe might, in Karen Sanchez-Eppler's terms, be guilty of "making their distinct exploitations appear identical," she departs from the "feminist-abolitionists" who are the subject of Sanchez-Eppler's critique as her novel forges a *literal* link between an actual slave and a woman that at once emphasizes the differences between them while insisting upon a mutually dependent connection between the two.

13. Lisa Whitney, "In the Shadow of *Uncle Tom's Cabin*: Stowe's Vision of Slavery from the Great Dismal Swamp," *New England Quarterly* 66 (1993): 555.

14. See Alfred L. Brophy, "Humanity, Utility, and Logic in Southern Legal Thought: Har-

riet Beecher Stowe's Vision in *Dred: A Tale of the Great Dismal Swamp*," *Boston University Law Review* 78 (1998): 1, 113–61; Gregg D. Crane, *Race, Citizenship, and Law in American Literature* (New York: Cambridge University Press, 2002); Mark V. Tushnet, *Slave Law in the American South: "State v. Mann" in History and Literature* (Lawrence: University Press of Kansas, 2003); Jeannine Marie DeLombard, "Representing the Slave: White Advocacy and Black Testimony in Harriet Beecher Stowe's *Dred*," *New England Quarterly* 75 (2002): 80–106; and Laura H. Korobkin, "Appropriating Law in Harriet Beecher Stowe's *Dred*," *Nineteenth-Century Literature* 62, no. 3 (2007): 380–406.

15. Stowe, *Uncle Tom's Cabin*, 233.

16. Stowe, *Uncle Tom's Cabin*, 64.

17. *Dred*, 14.

18. *Dred*, 38.

19. The status of marriage among slaves has been central to histories of the slave family. W. E. B. Du Bois, for instance, regarded the absence of legal marriage, legal family, and legal control over children as the essential feature of the slave family; W. E. B. Du Bois, *The Negro American Family* (Atlanta, 1908), 21–22. All views to the contrary, as E. Franklin Frazier points out in his pathbreaking history of "The Negro Slave Family," were efforts "by apologists of slavery to support their contention that the integrity of slave families was never violated"; E. Franklin Frazier, "The Negro Slave Family," *Journal of Negro History* 15, no. 2 (1930): 198. For more recent historical accounts of the formation of the slave family, see Herbert Gutman, *The Black Family in Slavery and Freedom, 1750–1925* (New York: Pantheon Books, 1976); Jacqueline Jones, *Labor of Love, Labor of Sorrow: Black Women, Work, and the Family from Slavery to the Present* (New York: Basic Books, 1985); Elizabeth Fox-Genovese, *Within the Plantation Household: Black and White Women of the Old South* (Chapel Hill: University of North Carolina Press, 1988); and Thavolia Glymph, *Out of the House of Bondage: The Transformation of the Plantation Household* (New York: Cambridge University Press, 2008).

20. *Dred*, 170.

21. *Dred*, 170.

22. American domesticity, for Stowe, is marked by cleanliness, order, and harmony. See Catherine Beecher and Harriet Beecher Stowe, *The American Woman's Home* (Hartford, Conn.: J. B. Ford, 1869), 458–59.

23. *Dred*, 38.

24. Two of the most famous accounts of sexual relations between slave owners and female slaves are found in Harriet Jacobs's 1861 memoir of a female slave and a diary entry of that same year by the white slave mistress, Mary Chesnutt. Though representing opposing positions, both accounts depict sex between white men and black women as the rape of female slaves by masters or other white men. Despite their different perspectives of slavery, both Jacobs and Chesnutt are highly critical of the tacit acceptance on the part of whites for this phenomenon of slave society.

25. *Dred*, 68.

26. *Dred*, 66.

27. *Dred*, 38.

28. *Dred*, 38.

29. Dylan C. Penningroth, *The Claims of Kinfolk: African American Property and Com-*

munity in the Nineteenth-Century South (Chapel Hill: University of North Carolina Press, 2003), 6

30. *Dred*, 61.

31. *Dred*, 61.

32. Dred, 20.

33. *Dred*, 10.

34. *Dred*, 80.

35. *Dred*, 129.

36. *Dred*, 140.

37. *Dred*, 140.

38. *Dred*, 140.

39. *Dred*, 141.

40. *Dred*, 145.

41. *Dred*, 144.

42. *Dred*, 39.

43. By the end of the novel, when they are finally free and living in Canada, Lisette is expecting a child.

44. *Dred*, 85.

45. *Dred*, 92.

46. *Dred*, 93.

47. *Dred*, 101.

48. *Dred*, 101.

49. *Dred*, 94.

50. *Dred*, 452.

51. *Dred*, 452.

52. *Dred*, 12–13.

53. *Dred*, 13.

54. *Dred*, 60.

55. See Peggy A. Rabkin, *Fathers to Daughters: The Legal Foundations of Female Emancipation* (Westport, Conn.: Greenwood Press, 1980), 3–5.

56. *Dred*, 131.

57. *Dred*, 131.

58. Joan Hedrick, *Harriet Beecher Stowe: A Life* (New York: Oxford University Press, 1994), 259.

59. For varying views on the failure of *Dred*, see Crane, *Race, Citizenship, and Law*, 178, and Alice C. Crozier, *The Novels of Harriet Beecher Stowe* (New York: Oxford University Press, 1969), 52–54. Part of the problem with the novel lies in the clash between its argument against slavery and the romance it develops between two slave masters. While the romance ends abruptly so that the antislavery plot dominates the narrative, its romance, according to these critics, depletes the political force of its antislavery message. For a discussion of the distinction between Stowe's antislavery politics in *Uncle Tom's Cabin* and *Dred*, see Whitney, "In the Shadow of *Uncle Tom's Cabin*," 553–56.

60. *Dred*, 31.

61. *Dred*, 32.

62. *Dred*, 32.

63. *Dred*, 21.
64. *Dred*, 547.
65. *Dred*, 548.
66. *Dred*, 548.
67. *Dred*, 92.
68. *Dred*, 174.
69. *Dred*, 174.
70. *Dred*, 174.
71. Stowe, *Uncle Tom's Cabin*, xiii.

Chapter 3: Free, Black, and Married

1. Frank Webb, *The Garies and Their Friends* (1857; Baltimore: Johns Hopkins University Press, 1997), 271. Hereafter cited by page number as *The Garies*.

2. *The Garies*, 271.

3. *The Garies*, 286.

4. *The Garies*, 4.

5. Cindy Weinstein, *Family, Kinship, and Sympathy in Nineteenth-Century American Literature* (New York: Cambridge University Press, 2005), 130.

6. Stephanie Coontz, *Marriage, a History: From Obedience to Intimacy or How Love Conquered Marriage* (New York: Viking, 2005), 15.

7. Coontz, *Marriage, a History*, 5.

8. Although Gary Nash's study of black Philadelphia provides important data concerning the number of marriages that occurred among free blacks in the late eighteenth and early nineteenth centuries, he offers few details of the legal and sentimental conventions upon which these marriages were based. His meticulous survey of church records offers a compelling connection between marriage and the former slaves' articulation of freedom. Similarly, Erica Armstrong Dunbar's study of free African American women in antebellum Philadelphia provides some evidence to suggest that for enslaved African American women, marriage to a free man held many advantages and could on occasion expedite emancipation. See Gary B. Nash, *Forging Freedom: The Formation of Philadelphia's Black Community, 1720–1840* (Cambridge, Mass.: Harvard University Press, 1988); and Erica Armstrong Dunbar, *A Fragile Freedom: African American Women and Emancipation in the Antebellum City* (New Haven, Conn.: Yale University Press, 2008), 31.

9. Harriet Beecher Stowe, *Uncle Tom's Cabin* (1852; repr., New York: Norton, 1999), xx.

10. For readings of Mary Webb's performances and accounts of her public life, see Susan F. Clark, "Solo Black Performance before the Civil War: Mrs. Stowe, Mrs. Webb, and 'The Christian Slave,'" *New Theatre Quarterly* 13, no. 52 (1997): 339–48; Eric Gardner, "Stowe Takes the Stage: Harriet Beecher Stowe's *The Christian Slave*," *Legacy* 15, no. 1 (1998): 78–84, and "'A Nobler End': Mary Webb and the Victorian Platform," *Nineteenth-Century Prose* 29, no. 1 (2002): 103–16.

11. While a few contemporary reviews appeared of *The Garies* in London, no reviews or notices of the novel appeared in the American mainstream or black press. See "Rev. of *The Garies and Their Friends* by Frank J. Webb," *Athanaeum* 1565 (1857): 1320; and "Rev. of *The Garies and Their Friends*, by Frank J. Webb," *Sunday Times*, September 27, 1857, 2.

12. See Samuel Otter, "Frank Webb's Still Life: Rethinking Literature and Politics through *The Garies and Their Friends*," *American Literary History* 20, no. 4 (2008): 728–52; and John Ernest, "Still Life, with Bones: A Response to Samuel Otter," *American Literary History* 20, no. 4 (2008): 753–65.

13. Ann duCille, *The Coupling Convention: Sex, Text, and Tradition in Black Women's Fiction* (New York: Oxford University Press, 1993), 14.

14. Frederick Douglass, *Narrative of the Life of Frederick Douglass, an American Slave, Written by Himself* (1845; New York: Signet, 1997), 111.

15. *The Garies*, 2.

16. *The Garies*, 133.

17. *The Garies*, 138.

18. William Wells Brown, *Clotel; or, The President's Daughter: A Narrative of Slave Life in the United States* (1853; repr., Boston: Bedford/St. Martin's, 2000), 100.

19. *The Garies*, 100.

20. See M. Giulia Fabi, *Passing and the Rise of the African American Novel* (Urbana: University of Illinois Press, 2001), 28; Blyden Jackson, *A History of Afro-American Literature* (Baton Rouge: Louisiana State University Press, 1989), 348; and Stephen Knadler, "Traumatized Racial Performativity: Passing in Nineteenth-Century African-American Testimonies," *Cultural Critique* 55 (Fall 2003): 77.

21. *The Garies*, 53.

22. *The Garies*, 53.

23. *The Garies*, 2.

24. *The Garies*, 101.

25. See Saidya V. Hartman, *Scenes of Subjection: Terror, Slavery, and Self-Making in Nineteenth-Century America* (New York: Oxford University Press, 1997), 67.

26. Nancy Cott, *Public Vows: A History of Marriage and the Nation* (Cambridge, Mass.: Harvard University Press, 2002), 43.

27. For a full account of anti-amalgamation legislation in the period, see Bruce Dorsey, *Reforming Men and Women: Gender in the Antebellum City* (Ithaca, N.Y.: Cornell University Press, 2002); and Leslie M. Harris, "From Abolitionist Amalgamators to 'Rulers of the Five Points': The Discourse of Interracial Sex and Reform in Antebellum New York City," in *Sex, Love, Race: Crossing Boundaries in North American History*, ed. Martha Hodes, 191–212 (New York: New York University Press, 1999).

28. *The Garies*, 137.

29. *The Garies*, 137.

30. *The Garies*, 138.

31. *The Garies*, 133.

32. *The Garies*, 100.

33. *The Garies*, 138.

34. *The Garies*, 135.

35. *The Garies*, 135.

36. *The Garies*, 125.

37. *The Garies*, 179.

38. *The Garies*, 135.

39. *The Garies*, 175–76.

40. *The Garies*, 16.

41. *The Garies*, 392.

42. Notably, Abraham Lincoln in a speech on the Dred Scott decision spoke quite openly and pointedly on the question of amalgamation. Lincoln went so far as to suggest that the problem of amalgamation is "much greater in the slave than in the free states. It is worthy of note too," Lincoln went on to say, "that among the free states those which make the colored man the nearest to equal the white, have, proportionably the fewest mulattoes the least of amalgamation." While Webb's novel does not mention explicitly the terms of the Dred Scott case to which Lincoln refers, my reading of the novel does suggest a strong parallel between Lincoln's response: "This very Dred Scott case affords a strong test as to which party most favors amalgamation" and what we might call the Republican position on amalgamation that Webb presents in his fiction. Abraham Lincoln, *The Language of Liberty: The Political Speeches and Writings of Abraham Lincoln*, ed. Joseph R. Fornieri (Washington, D.C: Regency, 2009), 221.

43. Deborah Gray White, *Ar'n't I a Woman: Female Slaves in the Plantation South* (New York: W. W. Norton, 1999), 58.

44. Harriet Jacobs, *Incidents in the Life of a Slave Girl, Written by Herself*, ed. Lydia Maria Child (Boston: Published for the Author, 1861), 306.

45. *The Garies*, 166.

46. *The Garies*, 202–3.

47. See Carla L. Peterson, *"Doers of the Word": African-American Women Speakers and Writers in the North (1830–1880)* (New Brunswick, N.J.: Rutgers University Press, 1995), 3–11.

48. *The Garies*, 205.

49. *The Garies*, 205.

50. For a discussion of the tensions between the conventions of "true womanhood" and the lives of enslaved women, see Hazel Carby, *Reconstructing Womanhood: The Emergence of the Afro-American Woman Novelist* (New York: Oxford University Press, 1987), 20–39.

51. *The Garies*, 205.

52. *The Garies*, 205.

53. *The Garies*, 205.

54. *The Garies*, 208.

55. *The Garies*, 238.

56. Robert Reid-Pharr, in his important reading of the novel, positions Esther as a black domestic heroine who earns her credentials "by reestablishing her role as literal guardian and caretaker of the hearth." By deploying the distinct language and ideology of American domesticity, Reid-Pharr argues that Webb has created a singular document of the nineteenth-century "black household." See Robert Reid-Pharr, *Conjugal Union: The Body, the House, and the Black American* (New York: Oxford University Press, 1999), 78–79. Extending Reid-Pharr's account of the novel's discourse of black domesticity, Anna Mae Duane draws a rather stark opposition between black women and white men. Duane contends that "Webb's insistence on empowering the black female body marks him as one of the earliest and strongest voices advocating an alternative distinctly black standard of womanhood." While Webb may indeed offer a standard for black womanhood, it is one that is nonetheless determined by the novel's male characters—a standard, I suggest,

that can best be understood by the marriage they form with one another. See Anna Mae Duane, "Rethinking Black Motherhood in Frank J. Webb's *The Garies and Their Friends*," *African American Review* 38, no. 2 (2004): 201–12.

57. *The Garies*, 205.

58. *The Garies*, 206.

59. *The Garies*, 207.

60. *The Garies*, 207.

61. *The Garies*, 335.

62. *The Garies*, 333.

63. *The Garies*, 333.

64. *The Garies*, 338–39.

65. *The Garies*, 342.

66. *The Garies*, 375–76.

67. *The Garies*, 392.

68. See Amy Kaplan, *The Anarchy of Empire in the Making of U.S. Culture* (Cambridge, Mass.: Harvard University Press, 2002), 45–46.

Chapter 4: "A Legally Unmarried Race"

1. Frances E. W. Harper, "The Two Offers," in *A Brighter Coming Day: A Frances Ellen Watkins Reader*, ed. Frances Smith Foster (1859; repr., New York: The Feminist Press at CUNY, 1990), 114. Subsequent references to this text will be to this edition, by page number, as "The Two Offers."

2. Catherine Maria Sedgwick, *Married or Single?*, 2 vols. (New York: Harper and Brothers, 1857). Like Harper's story, Sedgwick's novel questions the commonplace assumption that any marriage is preferable to a single life for women, and intersects with the discourse of women's rights.

3. "The Two Offers," 114.

4. "The Two Offers," 109.

5. Although Harper was a member of the *Anglo-African*'s editorial board and probably exerted some influence over the magazine's content, it was Thomas Hamilton's vision that it embodied. Hamilton described his publishing venture as "the dream of his youth . . . and the aim of his manhood." See William Loren Katz, "Preface," *Anglo-African Magazine Vol. 1—1859* (New York: Arno Press and the New York Times, 1968).

6. "The Two Offers," 114.

7. "The Two Offers," 106.

8. "The Two Offers," 109.

9. "The Two Offers," 114.

10. See Barbara Welter, "The Cult of True Womanhood, 1820–1860," in *Dimity Convictions: The American Woman in the Nineteenth Century* (Athens: Ohio State University Press, 1976), 41. For a discussion of how these conventions affected both the material condition and fictional representation of black women, see Hazel V. Carby, *Reconstructing Womanhood: The Emergence of the Afro-American Woman Novelist* (New York: Oxford University Press, 1987), 20–61.

11. In an essay that appeared the same year as "The Two Offers," Harper refers to herself as "an old maid . . . going about the country meddling with the slaveholders' business, and interfering with the their rights." See the *Anti-Slavery Bugle*, April 23, 1859.

12. Frances E. W. Harper, *Iola Leroy, or, Shadows Uplifted* (1892; repr., Boston: Beacon Press, 1987), 262.

13. "The Two Offers," 106.

14. See Hazel V. Carby, introduction to Frances E. W. Harper, *Iola Leroy* (1892; repr., Boston: Beacon Press, 1987), ix.

15. For an illuminating discussion of the role the Afro-Protestant press played in defining marriage in the everyday lives of nineteenth-century African Americans, see Frances Smith Foster, *'Til Death or Distance Do Us Part: Love and Marriage in African America* (New York: Oxford University Press, 2010), 56–70.

16. For a full account of this linking, see Karen Sanchez-Eppler, *Touching Liberty: Abolition, Feminism, and the Politics of the Body* (Berkeley: University of California Press, 1993), 14–49.

17. William Still, *The Underground Railroad* (Chicago: Johnson, 1970).

18. Still, *The Underground Railroad*, 785.

19. For examples of critical accounts of Harper's *Iola Leroy* in these terms, see Deborah McDowell, "'The Changing Same': Generational Connections and Black Women Novelists," in *Reading Black, Reading Feminist*, ed. Henry Louis Gates Jr. (New York: Penguin, 1990), 97; Gloria Naylor, "Love and Sex in the Afro-American Novel," *Yale Review* 78 (1989): 22; and Houston A. Baker Jr., *Workings of the Spirit: The Poetics of Afro-American Women's Writing* (Chicago: University of Chicago Press, 1991), 32.

20. Frances E. W. Harper, *Minnie's Sacrifice*, in *Minnie's Sacrifice; Sowing and Reaping; Trial and Triumph: Three Rediscovered Novels* (Boston: Beacon Press, 1994), 90.

21. "The Two Offers," 113.

22. Frances E. W. Harper, *Trial and Triumph*, in *Minnie's Sacrifice; Sowing and Reaping; Trial and Triumph: Three Rediscovered Novels*, 284.

23. *Trial and Triumph*, 285.

24. "The Two Offers."

25. Frances Smith Foster, introduction to Frances E. W. Harper, *A Brighter Coming Day: A Frances Ellen Watkins Harper Reader*, ed. Frances Smith Foster (1859; repr., New York: The Feminist Press at the City University of New York, 1990), 13.

26. Still, *The Underground Railroad*, 787.

27. Still, *The Underground Railroad*, 788.

28. Still, *The Underground Railroad*, 793.

29. Foster, introduction to *A Brighter Coming Day*, 18.

30. Harper, *A Brighter Coming Day*, 217.

31. For a full history of these material differences, see Jacqueline Jones, *Labor of Love, Labor of Sorrow: Black Women, Work, and the Family, From Slavery to the Present* (New York: Basic Books, 2010), 91–93.

32. Harper, *A Brighter Coming Day*, 218.

33. William Wells Brown, *Clotel; or, The President's Daughter: A Narrative of Slave Life in the United States* (1853; repr. Boston: Bedford/St. Martin's, 2000), 45.

34. Frances E. W. Harper, "Enlightened Motherhood: Pamphlet, Enlightened Mother-

hood: An Address by Mrs. Frances E. W. Harper before the Brooklyn Literary Society, November 15, 1892," in *A Brighter Coming Day*, ed. Frances Smith Foster (1859; repr., New York: The Feminist Press at CUNY, 1990), 285.

35. Cindy Weinstein, *Family, Kinship, and Sympathy in Nineteenth-Century American Literature* (New York: Cambridge University Press, 2005), 10–11.

36. Anna E. Dickinson, *What Answer?* with introduction by J. Matthew Gallman (1868; repr., New York: Humanity Books, 2003), 25.

37. *Minnie's Sacrifice*, 91.

38. That is not to say, however, that there is nothing to be gained from considering Harper's fiction in the context of other works, both fiction and nonfiction, that appeared in the *Christian Recorder*. In "Information Wanted: *The Curse of Caste, Minnie's Sacrifice*, and the *Christian Recorder*," Jean Lee Cole illuminates many aspects of Harper's novel by reading it both with and against Julia Collins's serial novel published in thirty-one installments in 1865. The differences between the authors are especially significant. Unlike Harper who was a well-known literary and political figure, Collins was virtually unknown and "died of tuberculosis before she finished the novel." Moreover, the form of their fictions diverge in crucial aspects. See Jean Lee Cole, "Information Wanted," *African American Review* 40, no. 4 (2006): 731–42, esp. 734.

39. It is worth noting here that Willie's lost arm and good intentions bear a striking resemblance to the rejected suitor, Dr. Gresham, of Harper's novel. Whereas in Dickinson's novel the lost arm indicates Willie's commitment to the cause of emancipation and helps to justify the interracial marriage, the opposite occurs in Harper's novel. Dr. Gresham's lost arm makes no difference to Iola, who remains steadfast in her commitment to the race and so refuses his proposal once again. For a particularly compelling reading of this episode in Harper's novel, see Geoffrey Sanborn, "Mother's Milk: Frances Harper and the Circulation of Blood," *Early Literary History* 72, no. 3 (2005): 691–715.

40. Dickinson had just published her first novel, *What Answer?* (1868), 259.

41. Dickinson, *What Answer?*, 282.

42. Dickinson, *What Answer?*, 315.

43. Dickinson, *What Answer?*, 209.

44. See Elizabeth Cady Stanton's "Rev. of *What Answer?*," *Revolution*, October 22, 1868. For a full discussion of Dickinson's political position in relation to African Americans and women, see J. Matthew Gallman, *America's Joan of Arc: The Life of Anna Elizabeth Dickinson* (New York: Oxford University Press, 2006), 80–93.

45. *Minnie's Sacrifice*, 5.

46. *Minnie's Sacrifice*, 12.

47. *Minnie's Sacrifice*, 15.

48. *Minnie's Sacrifice*, 33.

49. *Minnie's Sacrifice*, 81.

50. Hildegard Hoeller, "Self-Reliant Women in Frances Harper's Writings," *American Transcendental Quarterly* 3 (September 19, 2005): 207.

51. Jones, *Labor of Love, Labor of Sorrow*, 93–94, continues, "In contrast, black working women in the South had a more equal relationship with their husbands in the sense that the two partners were not separated by extremes of economic power or political rights; black men and women lacked both."

52. *Sowing and Reaping*, 103.

53. *Sowing and Reaping*, 154.

54. *Sowing and Reaping*, 159.

55. *Sowing and Reaping*, 174.

56. *Sowing and Reaping*, 96.

57. *Sowing and Reaping*, 105.

58. *Sowing and Reaping*, 166.

59. Harper, *A Brighter Coming Day*, 285.

60. *Iola Leroy*, 246.

61. *Iola Leroy*, 261.

62. *Iola Leroy*, 117.

63. *Iola Leroy*, 271.

64. P. Gabrielle Foreman, *Activist Sentiments: Reading Black Women in the Nineteenth Century* (Urbana: University of Illinois Press, 2009), 73.

65. *Iola Leroy*, 26.

66. *Iola Leroy*, 28.

67. *Iola Leroy*, 275.

Chapter 5: Wedded to Race

1. Charles W. Chesnutt, "Uncle Wellington's Wives," in *Stories, Novels and Essays* (New York: Library Classics of the United States, 2002), hereafter cited by page number.

2. "Uncle Wellington's Wives," 219.

3. "Uncle Wellington's Wives," 219.

4. "Uncle Wellington's Wives," 219.

5. "Uncle Wellington's Wives," 219.

6. See Ann duCille, *The Coupling Convention: Sex, Text, and Tradition in Black Women's Fiction* (New York: Oxford University Press, 1993), 2.

7. "Uncle Wellington's Wives," 213.

8. See Nancy F. Cott, *Public Vows: A History of Marriage and the Nation* (Cambridge, Mass.: Harvard University Press, 2000), 33; and Margaret A. Burnham, "An Impossible Marriage: Slave Law and Family Law," *Law and Inequality* 5 (1987): 187–90.

9. Herbert Gutman provides one of the first and most enlightening investigations into the nature of slave-marriages and their ability to withstand enforced separations both during and after the Civil War. See Herbert Gutman, *The Black Family in Slavery and Freedom, 1750–1925* (New York: Vintage Books, 1976), 3–37.

10. Cott, *Public Vows*, 84.

11. "Uncle Wellington's Wives," 252.

12. "Uncle Wellington's Wives," 234.

13. "Uncle Wellington's Wives," 213.

14. See Nancy Bentley, "The Strange Career of Love and Slavery: Chesnutt, Engels, Masoch," *American Literary History* 17, no. 3 (2005): 463.

15. Bentley, "The Strange Career of Love and Slavery," 463.

16. Charles W. Chesnutt, *The Marrow of Tradition*, in *Stories, Novels and Essays* (New York: Library Classics of the United States, 2002), 674, hereafter cited by page number.

17. "Uncle Wellington's Wives," 231.

18. "Uncle Wellington's Wives," 208.

19. Charles W. Chesnutt, "The Wife of His Youth," in *Stories, Novels and Essays* (New York: Library Classics of the United States, 2002), 101, hereafter cited by page number.

20. "The Wife of His Youth," 101.

21. "The Wife of His Youth," 103.

22. "The Wife of His Youth," 105.

23. "The Wife of His Youth," 103.

24. "The Wife of His Youth," 102.

25. "The Wife of His Youth," 105.

26. Charles Duncan, "Telling Genealogy: Notions of Family in *The Wife of His Youth*," in *Critical Essays on Charles W. Chesnutt*, ed. Joseph R. McElrath Jr. (New York: G. K. Hall, 1999), 282.

27. "The Wife of His Youth," 110.

28. "The Wife of His Youth," 103.

29. Henry Wonham, "What Is a Black Author?: A Review of Recent Charles Chesnutt Studies," *American Literary History* 18, no. 4 (2006): 831.

30. Charles W. Chesnutt, "The Future American," in *Stories, Novels and Essays* (New York: Library Classics of the United States, 2002), 840, hereafter cited by page number.

31. See duCille, *The Coupling Convention*, 16.

32. "The Wife of His Youth," 112.

33. "The Wife of His Youth," 101.

34. Quoted in Helen M. Chesnutt, *Charles Waddell Chesnutt: Pioneer of the Color Line* (Chapel Hill: University of North Carolina Press, 1952), 98.

35. Chesnutt, *Charles Waddell Chesnutt*, 98.

36. Chesnutt, *Charles Waddell Chesnutt*, 102.

37. duCille, *The Coupling Convention*, 16.

38. "The Future American," 874.

39. "The Future American," 849.

40. "The Future American," 846.

41. "The Future American," 850.

42. "The Future American," 850.

43. "The Future American," 859.

44. Sally Ann Ferguson, "Chesnutt's Genuine Blacks and Future Americans," *MELUS* 15, no. 3 (Autumn 1988): 109; and Matthew Wilson, *Whiteness in the Novels of Charles W. Chesnutt* (Jackson: University of Mississippi Press, 2004), 11.

45. Samira Kawash, *Dislocating the Color Line: Identity, Hybridity, and Singularity in African-American Narrative* (Stanford, Calif.: Stanford University Press, 1997), 88.

46. *The Marrow of Tradition*, 535.

47. *The Marrow of Tradition*, 506.

48. *The Marrow of Tradition*, 506.

49. *The Marrow of Tradition*, 506.

50. *The Marrow of Tradition*, 506.

51. *The Marrow of Tradition*, 507.

52. *The Marrow of Tradition*, 507.

53. *The Marrow of Tradition*, 508.

54. *The Marrow of Tradition*, 669.

55. Michael Warner, *Public and Counterpublics* (New York: Zone Books, 2002), 18.

56. *The Marrow of Tradition*, 669.

57. *The Marrow of Tradition*, 669.

58. *The Marrow of Tradition*, 717.

59. *The Marrow of Tradition*, 718.

60. *The Marrow of Tradition*, 718.

61. *The Marrow of Tradition*, 671.

62. *The Marrow of Tradition*, 717.

63. "The Wife of His Youth," 107.

64. Amy Dru Stanley, *From Bondage to Contract: Wage Labor, Marriage, and the Market in the Age of Slave Emancipation* (Cambridge: Cambridge University Press, 1998), 35.

65. Eric J. Sundquist, *To Wake the Nations: Race in the Making of American Literature* (Cambridge, Mass.: Harvard University Press, 1993), 301.

66. *The Marrow of Tradition*, 722.

67. "The Wife of His Youth," 105.

68. "The Wife of His Youth," 109.

69. "The Wife of His Youth," 107.

70. "The Wife of His Youth," 108.

71. "The Wife of His Youth," 110.

72. "The Wife of His Youth," 112.

73. Cott, *Public Vows*, 1.

74. "The Wife of His Youth," 112.

75. Claudia Tate, "Allegories of Black Female Desire; or, Rereading Nineteenth Century Sentimental Narratives of Black Female Authority," in *Changing Our Own Words: Essays on Criticism, Theory, and Writing by Black Women*, ed. Cheryl A. Wall (New Brunswick, N.J.: Rutgers University Press, 1989), 103.

76. Charles W. Chesnutt, "A Matter of Principle," in *Stories, Novels and Essays* (New York: Library Classics of the United States, 2002), 149, hereafter cited by page number.

77. "A Matter of Principle," 150.

78. "A Matter of Principle," 151.

79. "A Matter of Principle," 151.

80. "A Matter of Principle," 167.

81. "A Matter of Principle," 152.

82. Charles W. Chesnutt, "Her Virginia Mammy," in *Stories, Novels and Essays* (New York: Library Classics of the United States, 2002), 116, hereafter cited by page number.

83. "Her Virginia Mammy," 116.

84. "Her Virginia Mammy," 116.

85. "Her Virginia Mammy," 117.

86. "Her Virginia Mammy," 117.

87. "Her Virginia Mammy," 125.

88. "Her Virginia Mammy," 125.

89. "Her Virginia Mammy," 123.

90. "Her Virginia Mammy," 115.

91. "Her Virginia Mammy," 117.

92. Charles W. Chesnutt, "Cicely's Dream," in *Stories, Novels and Essays* (New York: Library Classics of the United States, 2002), 170, hereafter cited by page number.

93. "Cicely's Dream," 170.

94. "Cicely's Dream," 172.

95. "Cicely's Dream," 173.

96. Chesnutt is typically characterized as a writer in the realist tradition and his contributions to literary realism continue to dominate critical discussions of his fiction. See, for example, Ryan Simmons, *Chesnutt and Realism: A Study of the Novels* (Tuscaloosa: University of Alabama Press, 2006), 1–11.

97. Quoted in Chesnutt, *Charles Waddell Chesnutt*, 115.

98. Ross Posnock, *Color and Culture: Black Writers and the Making of the Modern Intellectual* (Cambridge, Mass.: Harvard University Press, 1998), 5.

Conclusion. Reading Hannah Crafts in the Twenty-First Century

1. Hannah Crafts, *The Bondwoman's Narrative* (New York: Warner Books, 2002), xi.

2. Eric Gardner, *Unexpected Places: Relocating Nineteenth-Century African American Literature* (Jackson: University Press of Mississippi, 2009), 175.

3. Crafts, *The Bondwoman's Narrative*, 212.

4. Crafts, *The Bondwoman's Narrative*, 246.

5. Crafts, *The Bondwoman's Narrative*, 21.

6. Crafts, *The Bondwoman's Narrative*, 122.

7. Crafts, *The Bondwoman's Narrative*, 123.

8. Crafts, *The Bondwoman's Narrative*, 146.

9. Crafts, *The Bondwoman's Narrative*, 146.

10. Crafts, *The Bondwoman's Narrative*, 148.

11. Crafts, *The Bondwoman's Narrative*, 246.

Selected Bibliography

Andrews, William. *To Tell a Free Story: The First Century of Afro-American Autobiography, 1760–1855*. Urbana: University of Illinois Press, 1988.

Aptheker, Herbert, ed. *A Documentary History of the Negro People in the United States*. New York: Citadel, 1969.

Baker Jr., Houston A. *Workings of the Spirit: The Poetics of Afro-American Women's Writing*. Chicago: University of Chicago Press, 1991.

Beecher, Catherine, and Harriet Beecher Stowe. *The American Woman's Home*. Hartford, Conn.: J. B. Ford, 1869.

Bentley, Nancy. "The Strange Career of Love and Slavery: Chesnutt, Engels, Masoch." *American Literary History* 17, no. 3 (2005): 460–85.

Bibb, Henry. *Narrative of the Life and Adventures of Henry Bibb, an American Slave, Written by Himself*. 1849; repr., Madison: University of Wisconsin Press, 2001.

Blackstone, William. *Commentaries on the Laws of England*, vol. 1. Oxford: Clarendon Press, 1770.

Blassingame, John. *The Slave Community: Plantation Life in the Antebellum South*. Oxford: Oxford University Press, 1979.

Brophy, Alfred L. "Humanity, Utility, and Logic in Southern Legal Thought: Harriet Beecher Stowe's Vision in *Dred: A Tale of the Great Dismal Swamp*." *Boston University Law Review* 78 (1998): 113–61.

Brown, William Wells. *The Autobiographies of William Wells Brown*. Ed. William Andrews. Columbia: University of Missouri Press, 2003.

———. *The Black Man: His Antecedents, His Genius, and His Achievements*. New York: T. Hamilton, 1863.

———. *Clotel; or, The President's Daughter*. 1853; repr., Boston: Bedford/St. Martin's, 2000.

———. *Clotelle, or, The Colored Heroine*. Boston: Lee and Shepard, 1867.

———. *Memoir of William Wells Brown, an American Bondman, Written by Himself*. Boston: Boston Anti-Slavery Office, 1859.

———. *My Southern Home; or, the South and Its People*. Boston: H. G. Brown, 1880.

———. *Narrative of William W. Brown, a Fugitive Slave, Written by Himself.* 1847; repr., New York: Harper and Row, 1969.

———. *The Negro in the American Rebellion: His Heroism and His Fidelity.* 1867; repr., Chicago: Chicago Distribution Center, 2003.

———. *William Wells Brown: A Reader.* Ed. Ezra Greenspan. Athens: University of Georgia Press, 2008.

———. *The Works of William Wells Brown: Using His "Strong and Manly Voice."* New York: Oxford University Press, 2006.

Carby, Hazel V. *Reconstructing Womanhood: The Emergence of the Afro-American Woman Novelist.* New York: Oxford University Press, 1987.

Castronovo, Russ. *Fathering the Nation: American Genealogies of Slavery and Freedom.* Berkeley: University of California Press, 1995.

Chesnutt, Charles W. *Stories, Novels and Essays.* New York: Library Classics of the United States, 2002.

Chesnutt, Helen M. *Charles Waddell Chesnutt: Pioneer of the Color Line.* Chapel Hill: University of North Carolina Press, 1952.

Child, Lydia Maria. *An Appeal in Favor of That Class of Americans Called Africans.* 1833; repr., New York: Arno Press, 1968.

———. *Fact and Fiction: A Collection of Stories.* New York: C. S. Francis, 1846.

———. *The History of the Condition of Women, in Various Ages and Nations.* Boston: Otis, Broaders, 1843.

———. *A Lydia Maria Child Reader.* Ed. Carolyn L. Karcher. Durham, N.C.: Duke University Press, 1997.

Christian, George L., and Frank W. Christian. "Slave-Marriages." *Virginia Law Journal* 1, no. 11 (1877): 641–52.

Clark, Susan F. "Solo Black Performance before the Civil War: Mrs. Stowe, Mrs. Webb, and 'The Christian Slave.'" *New Theatre Quarterly* 13, no. 52 (1997): 339–48.

Cole, Jean Lee. "Information Wanted: *The Curse of Caste, Minnie's Sacrifice,* and the *Christian Recorder.*" *African American Review* 40, no. 4 (2006): 731–42.

Coontz, Stephanie. *Marriage, a History: From Obedience to Intimacy or How Love Conquered Marriage.* New York: Viking, 2005.

Cornell, Drucilla. *Imaginary Domain.* New York: Routledge, 1988.

Cott, Nancy. *Public Vows: A History of Marriage and the Nation.* Cambridge, Mass.: Harvard University Press, 2002.

Craft, William. *Running a Thousand Miles for Freedom: The Escape of William and Ellen Craft from Slavery.* 1860; repr., Athens: University of Georgia Press, 1999.

Crafts, Hannah. *The Bondwoman's Narrative.* New York: Warner Books, 2002.

Crane, Gregg D. *Race, Citizenship, and Law in American Literature.* New York: Cambridge University Press, 2002.

Crozier, Alice C. *The Novels of Harriet Beecher Stowe.* New York: Oxford University Press, 1969.

DeLombard, Jeannine Marie. "Representing the Slave: White Advocacy and Black Testimony in Harriet Beecher Stowe's *Dred.*" *New England Quarterly* 75 (2002): 80–106.

Dickinson, Anna E. *What Answer?* 1868; repr., New York: Humanity Books, 2003.

Dorsey, Bruce. *Reforming Men and Women: Gender in the Antebellum City.* Ithaca, N.Y.: Cornell University Press, 2002.

Dorsey, Peter A. "De-Authorizing Slavery: Realism in Stowe's *Uncle Tom's Cabin* and Brown's *Clotel.*" *ESQ: A Journal of the American Renaissance* 41 (1995): 256–88.

Douglass, Frederick. *My Bondage and My Freedom.* New York: Miller, Orton, and Mulligan, 1855.

———. *Narratives of the Life of Frederick Douglass, an American Slave, Written by Himself.* New York: Signet, 1997.

Duane, Anna Mae. "Rethinking Black Motherhood in Frank J. Webb's *The Garies and Their Friends.*" *African American Review* 38, no. 2 (2004): 201–12.

Du Bois, W. E. B. *The Negro American Family.* Atlanta: Atlanta University Press, 1908.

duCille, Ann. *The Coupling Convention: Sex, Text, and Tradition in Black Women's Fiction.* New York: Oxford University Press, 1993.

———. "Where in the World Is William Wells Brown? Thomas Jefferson, Sally Hemings, and the DNA of African-American Literary History." *American Literary History* 12, no. 3 (2000): 443–62.

Dunbar, Erica Armstrong. *A Fragile Freedom: African American Women and Emancipation in the Antebellum City.* New Haven, Conn.: Yale University Press, 2008.

Duncan, Charles. "Telling Genealogy: Notions of Family in *The Wife of His Youth.*" In *Critical Essays on Charles W. Chesnutt,* ed. Joseph R. McElrath Jr. New York: G. K. Hall, 1999.

Ernest, John. *Liberation Historiography: African American Writers and the Challenge of History, 1794–1861.* Chapel Hill: University of North Carolina Press, 2004.

———. *Resistance and Reformation in Nineteenth-Century African-American Literature: Brown, Wilson, Jacobs, Delany, Douglass, and Harper.* Jackson: University Press of Mississippi, 1998.

———. "Still Life, with Bones: A Response to Samuel Otter." *American Literary History* 20, no. 4 (2008): 753–65.

Fabi, M. Giulia. *Passing and the Rise of the African American Novel.* Urbana: University of Illinois Press, 2001.

———. "The 'Unguarded Expressions of the Feelings of Negroes': Gender, Slave Resistance of *Clotel.*" *African American Review* 27 (1993): 639–54.

Farrison, William Edward. *William Wells Brown: Author, Reformer.* Chicago: University of Chicago Press, 1969.

Ferguson, Sally Ann. "Chesnutt's Genuine Blacks and Future Americans." *MELUS* 15, no. 3 (Autumn 1988): 101–19.

Foreman, P. Gabrielle. *Activist Sentiments: Reading Black Women in the Nineteenth Century.* Urbana: University of Illinois Press, 2009.

Foster, Frances Smith. *Love and Marriage in Early African America.* Boston: Northeastern University Press, 2007.

———. *'Til Death or Distance Do Us Part: Love and Marriage in African America.* New York: Oxford University Press, 2010.

Fox-Genovese, Elizabeth. *Within the Plantation Household: Black and White Women of the Old South.* Chapel Hill: University of North Carolina Press, 1988.

Franke, Katherine. "Becoming a Citizen: Post-Bellum Regulation of African American Marriage." *Yale Journal of Law and the Humanities* 11 (1992): 251–309.

Frazier, E. Franklin. "The Negro Slave Family." *Journal of Negro History* 15, no. 2 (1930): 198–259.

Gardner, Eric. "'A Nobler End': Mary Webb and the Victorian Platform." *Nineteenth-Century Prose* 29, no. 1 (2002): 103–16.

———. "Stowe Takes the Stage: Harriet Beecher Stowe's *The Christian Slave*." *Legacy* 15, no. 1 (1998): 78–84.

———. *Unexpected Places: Relocating Nineteenth-Century African American Literature.* Jackson: University Press of Mississippi, 2009.

Gayle, Addison. *The Way of the New World: The Black Novel in America.* New York: Anchor Press, 1975.

Genovese, Eugene D. *Roll, Jordan, Roll: The World the Slaves Made.* New York: Pantheon Books, 1974.

Glymph, Thavolia. *Out of the House of Bondage: The Transformation of the Plantation Household.* New York: Cambridge University Press, 2008.

Griggs, Sutton E. *Imperium in Imperio.* 1899; repr., New York: Modern Library, 2003.

Grimké, Sarah. *The Female Experience: An American Documentary.* Ed. Gerda Lerner. New York: Oxford University Press, 1992.

———. *Letters on the Equality of the Sexes and the Condition of Women.* Boston: I. Knapp, 1838.

Guillory, Monique. "Under One Roof: The Sins and Sanctity of the New Orleans Quadroon Balls." In *Race Consciousness,* eds. Judith Jackson Fossett and Jeffrey A. Tucker. New York: New York University Press, 1997.

Gutman, Herbert. *The Black Family in Slavery and Freedom, 1750–1925.* New York: Pantheon Books, 1976.

Hammerton, James. *Cruelty and Companionship: Conflict in Nineteenth-Century Married Life.* New York: Routledge, 1992.

Harper, Frances E. W. *A Brighter Coming Day: A Frances Ellen Watkins Harper Reader.* Ed. Frances Smith Foster. 1859; repr., New York: The Feminist Press at CUNY, 1990.

———. *Iola Leroy, or, Shadows Uplifted.* 1892; repr., Boston: Beacon Press, 1987.

———. *Minnie's Sacrifice; Sowing and Reaping; Trial and Triumph: Three Rediscovered Novels.* Boston: Beacon Press, 1994.

Harris, Leslie M. "From Abolitionist Amalgamators to 'Rulers of the Five Points': The Discourse of Interracial Sex and Reform in Antebellum New York City." In *Sex, Love, Race: Crossing Boundaries in North American History.* Ed. Martha Hodes, 191–212. New York: New York University Press, 1999.

Hartman, Saidya V. *Scenes of Subjection: Terror, Slavery, and Self-Making in Nineteenth-Century America.* New York: Oxford University Press, 1997.

Hartog, Hendrik. *Man and Wife in America.* Cambridge, Mass.: Harvard University Press, 2000.

Hedrick, Joan. *Harriet Beecher Stowe: A Life.* New York: Oxford University Press, 1994.

Hodes, Martha. *White Women, Black Men: Illicit Sex in the Nineteenth-Century South.* New Haven, Conn.: Yale University Press, 1997.

Holcombe, Lee. *Wives and Property: Reform of the Married Women's Property Law in Nineteenth-Century England.* Toronto: University of Toronto Press, 1983.

Jackson, Blyden. *A History of Afro-American Literature.* Baton Rouge: Louisiana State University Press, 1989.

Jacobs, Harriet. *Incidents in the Life of a Slave Girl, Written by Herself.* 1861; repr., New York: Penguin, 2000.

Jones, Jacqueline. *Labor of Love, Labor of Sorrow: Black Women, Work, and the Family from Slavery to the Present*. New York: Basic Books, 2010.

Joyner, Charles. *Down by the Riverside: A South Carolina Slave Community*. Urbana: University of Illinois Press, 1984.

Kaplan, Amy. *The Anarchy of Empire in the Making of U.S. Culture*. Cambridge, Mass.: Harvard University Press, 2002.

Karcher, Carolyn L. "Rape, Murder and Revenge in 'Slavery's Pleasant Homes': Lydia Maria Child's Antislavery Fiction and the Limits of Genre." *Women's Studies International Forum* 9, no. 4 (1986).

Katz, William Loren, ed. *The Anglo-African Magazine*. 1859; repr., New York: Arno Press, 1968.

Kawash, Samira. *Dislocating the Color Line: Identity, Hybridity, and Singularity in African-American Narratives*. Stanford, Calif.: Stanford University Press, 1997.

Kent, James. *Commentaries on American Law*. New York: D. Halsted, 1826.

Knadler, Stephen. "Traumatized Racial Performativity: Passing in Nineteenth-Century African-American Testimonies." *Cultural Critique* 55 (Fall 2003): 63–100.

Korobkin, Laura H. "Appropriating Law in Harriet Beecher Stowe's *Dred*." *Nineteenth-Century Literature* 62, no. 3 (2007): 380–406.

Morrison, Toni. *Playing in the Dark: Whiteness and the Literary Imagination*. New York: Vintage, 1993.

Nabers, Deak. "The Problem of Revolution in the Age of Slavery." *Representations* 91 (2005): 84–108.

Nash, Gary. *Forging Freedom: The Formation of Philadelphia's Black Community, 1720–1840*. Cambridge, Mass.: Harvard University Press, 1988.

Naylor, Gloria. "Love and Sex in the Afro-American Novel." *Yale Review* 78 (1989): 19–31.

Otter, Samuel. "Frank Webb's Still Life: Rethinking Literature and Politics through *The Garies and Their Friends*." *American Literary History* 20, no. 4 (2008): 728–52.

Penningroth, Dylan C. *The Claims of Kinfolk: African American Property and Community in the Nineteenth-Century South*. Chapel Hill: University of North Carolina Press, 2003.

Peterson, Carla L. *"Doers of the Word": African-American Women Speakers and Writers in the North, 1830–1880*. New Brunswick, N.J.: Rutgers University Press, 1995.

Posnock, Ross. *Color and Culture: Black Writers and the Making of the Modern Intellectual*. Cambridge, Mass.: Harvard University Press, 1998.

Rabkin, Peggy A. *Fathers to Daughters: The Legal Foundations of Female Emancipation*. Westport, Conn.: Greenwood Press, 1980.

Reid-Pharr, Robert. *Conjugal Union: The Body, the House, and the Black American*. New York: Oxford University Press, 1999.

Rushdy, Ashraf. *Neo-Slave Narratives: Studies in the Social Logic of a Literary Form*. New York: Oxford University Press, 1999.

Sanchez-Eppler, Karen. *Touching Liberty: Abolition, Feminism, and the Politics of the Body*. Berkeley: University of California Press, 1993.

Schweninger, Lee. "*Clotel* and the Historicity of the Anecdote." *MELUS* 24 (1999): 21–36.

Sedgwick, Catherine Maria. *Married or Single?* New York: Harper and Brothers, 1857.

Simmons, Ryan. *Chesnutt and Realism: A Study of the Novels*. Tuscaloosa: University of Alabama Press, 2006.

Sollors, Werner. "A British Mercenary and American Abolitionists: Literary Retellings from 'Inkle and Yarico' and John Gabriel Steadman to Lydia Maria Child and William Wells Brown." In *Formation of Cultural Identity in the English-Speaking World*, ed. Jochen Achilles and Carmen Birkle. Heidelberg: Universitätsverlag C. Winter, 1998.

Stanley, Amy Dru. *From Bondage to Contract: Wage Labor, Marriage, and the Market in the Age of Slave Emancipation*. Cambridge: Cambridge University Press, 1998.

Stanton, Elizabeth Cady. *History of Woman Suffrage*, vols. 1–2. 1861–1881; repr., Salem, N.H.: Ayer, 1985.

Still, William. *The Underground Railroad*. Chicago: Johnson, 1970.

Stowe, Harriet Beecher. *Dred: A Tale of the Great Dismal Swamp*. 1856; repr., New York: Penguin, 2000.

———. *The Minister's Wooing*. 1859; repr., London: Penguin, 1999.

———. *Uncle Tom's Cabin*. 1852; repr., New York: Norton, 1999.

Sundquist, Eric J. *To Wake the Nations: Race in the Making of American Literature*. Cambridge, Mass.: Harvard University Press, 1993.

Tate, Claudia. *Domestic Allegories of Political Desire: The Black Heroine's Text at the Turn of the Century*. New York: Oxford University Press, 1992.

Tocqueville, Alexis de. *Democracy in America*. New York: Knopf, 1945.

Tompkins, Jane. *Sentimental Designs: The Cultural Work of American Fiction, 1790–1860*. New York: Oxford University Press, 1985.

Tushnet, Mark V. *Slave Law in the American South: "State v. Mann" in History and Literature*. Lawrence: University Press of Kansas, 2003.

Wall, Cheryl A. *Changing Our Own Words: Essays on Criticism, Theory, and Writing by Black Women*. New Brunswick, N.J.: Rutgers University Press, 1989.

Warner, Michael. *Public and Counterpublics*. New York: Zone Books, 2002.

Webb, Frank. *The Garies and Their Friends*. 1857; repr., Baltimore: Johns Hopkins University Press, 1997.

Weinstein, Cindy. *Family, Kinship, and Sympathy in Nineteenth-Century American Literature*. New York: Cambridge University Press, 2005.

Welter, Barbara. "The Cult of True Womanhood, 1820–1860." In *Dimity Convictions: The American Woman in the Nineteenth Century*. Athens: Ohio State University Press, 1976.

West, Emily. *Chains of Love: Slave Couples in Antebellum South Carolina*. Urbana: University of Illinois Press, 2004.

White, Deborah Gray. *Ar'n't I a Woman: Female Slaves in the Plantation South*. New York: W. W. Norton, 1999.

Whitney, Lisa. "In the Shadow of *Uncle Tom's Cabin*: Stowe's Vision of Slavery from the Great Dismal Swamp." *New England Quarterly* 66 (1993): 552–69.

Wilson, Matthew. *Whiteness in the Novels of Charles W. Chesnutt*. Jackson: University of Mississippi Press, 2004.

Wonham, Henry. "What Is a Black Author?: A Review of Recent Charles Chesnutt Studies." *American Literary History* 18, no. 4 (2006): 829–35.

Index

amalgamation, 89, 91–93, 124n42
Anthony, Susan B., 71
antislavery movement: Brown writings on, 21; Enlightenment philosophy as antislavery foundation, 26–28; influence on women's rights movement, 43; legal slave marriage associated with, 55

Beecher, Catherine, 33
Bentley, Nancy, 86, 100–101
Bibb, Henry, 1
Blackstone, William, 32
Blackwell, Henry R., 118n64
Blassingame, John, 4, 8
Breckenridge, Robert J., 31
Brown, William Wells: autobiographical writings of, 17, 116n9; on forced marriage, 108–9; on forced separation, 21–22, 73; as fugitive slave, 29, 109; on legal marriage, 54; marriages of, 10, 17; origin of personal name, 18; sentimental discourse in, 3, 113–14n7; on slave marriage as ideal, 2–4, 48; on slave-owner conjugal relations, 37. Works: *The Narrative of the Life of William W. Brown* (1847), 15, 17, 23; "The American Slave-Trade" (1848), 21; *Clotel* (1853), see main entry *Clotel*; *Clotelle* (1867), 30; *My Southern Home* (1880), 17

Cary, Mary Ann Shadd, 58
Castronovo, Russ, 116n9
Chesnutt, Charles W.: on the "color line," 84–85, 87–88, 94–95, 105–6; on marriage as racial affiliation, 97–99, 104–5, 107; on mixed-race marriages, 85–86, 97–98; racial amalgamation theory, 89, 91–93; as realist writer, 131n96; on segregation, 94–95, 97; on slave-marriage legitimation, 13, 84. Works: "What Is a White Man?" (1889), 89; "Cicely's Dream" (1899), 103–4; *The Conjure Woman* (1899), 97–98, 105; "Her Virginia Mammy" (1899), 101–3; "A Matter of Principle" (1899), 100–101; "Uncle Wellington's Wives" (1899), 83–88, 93, 112; "The Wife of His Youth" (1899), 88–91, 97–99, 102; "The Future American" (1900), 89, 92; *The House behind the Cedars* (1900), 87; *The Marrow of Tradition* (1901), 86–87, 93–94
Chesnutt, Mary, 120n24
Child, Lydia Maria: on coverture, 6; on legal marriage, 9, 54; on sexual abuse by slaveholders, 3, 7; slave marriage in, 6–7; on women's rights, 33. Works: "The Quadroons" (1842), 25; "Slavery's Pleasant Homes" (1843), 6–7
Christian, Frank W., 119n2

Christian, George L., 119n2

Christianity: as basis for marriage, 9, 73, 111; Christian "ideal beings" in Harper, 67, 69, 77–78; justification of slavery in, 26–27, 31; religious acceptance of slave bigamy/adultery, 22–23; sanctioned marriage as barrier to authentic love, 25–26

Clotel (Brown): antislavery theme in, 26–27, 51; edition of 1867, 30; religious foundation of marriage in, 22–23; reunion of George and Mary Green, 28–29; slave marriage depiction in, 2–3, 16–18, 23–25, 50–51

Cole, Jean Lee, 127n38

Collins, Julia, 127n38

Colson v. Quander (legitimation), 119n2

concubinage, 31–32, 52

Coontz, Stephanie, 20, 48

Cornell, Drucilla, 3

Cott, Nancy, 53, 85

coverture: defined, 6; debt and inheritance laws, 71; Harper critique of, 12–13, 64–65; legal principles of, 28, 32–33; women's rights and, 43. *See also* law; marriage; property

Craft, William and Ellen, 8–9, 28, 110

Crafts, Hannah (*The Bondwoman's Narrative*, 1850s), 108–12

Crane, Gregg, 34

Delany, Martin, 58, 65

Dickens, Charles, 24–25

Dickinson, Anna E. (*What Answer?* 1868), 74–75, 127n39

Douglass, Anna, 15

Douglass, Frederick: on marriage as token of freedom, 49–50; on nonfiction as an obligation, 4; women's scholarship as complement for, 58. Works: *Narrative of the Life of Frederick Douglass* (1845), 15, 49–50; *My Bondage and My Freedom* (1855), 15

Dred (Stowe): as antislavery novel, 31–34, 41–46, 121n59; critique of legal marriage, 32–34, 39–42, 44–46, 119n9, 119n12; critique of property, 35–39;

legitimacy of slave marriage in, 119n2; slave marriage as ideal in, 10, 33–34, 41–42, 46, 111

Duane, Anna Mae, 124–25n56

Du Bois, W. E. B., 105, 120n19

duCille, Ann: on the consequences of legitimation, 84, 85; on marriage in African-American literature, 49; on the Sally Hemings DNA tests, 115n35; on slave marriage as resistance, 8, 18; on "unreal estates," 115n30

Dunbar, Erica Armstrong, 122n8

Duncan, Charles, 89

Ellison, Ralph, 92–93

emancipation. *See* freedom

Ernest, John, 5, 21

escape: Dismal Swamp escape in *Dred*, 42; feigned marital submission as strategy for, 16–17, 109; forced marriage as impetus for, 108–9; as marriage issue, 2, 9, 16–17, 28, 110–11. *See also* freedom

feminism. *See* women

fiction: *The Bondwoman's Narrative* as slave fiction, 108; conceptualization of slave marriage, 1–2; Garie-Winston fictional marriage, 50; "happy ending" marriage narrative, 29, 48, 61–63, 80–81, 87, 102, 109; Harper as fiction writer, 68; in historical research, 4–5; ironic property in *Dred*, 35–38; slave-marriage ideal depicted in, 18; "strategic lying" in Brown, 17; "unreal estate" fictional realm in Brown, 115n30; Victorian romantic subjects as fictional slave-marriage models, 29

Foreman, Gabrielle P., 81

Forten, Charlotte, 58

Foster, Frances Smith, 67

Fox-Genovese, Elizabeth, 4

Frazier, E. Franklin, 120n19

free black marriage: defined, 48–49; freedom as problem for, 10; Harper critique of, 72–74; historical studies of, 122n8; legitimation of slave marriages, 13, 84, 119n2; "political desire" in, 12;

prohibition of mixed-race marriages, 85–89, 89–90, 101–3; public meaning as problem for, 11; as racial affiliation, 53–63, 97–99, 100, 107. *See also* freedom; legal marriage; Reconstruction era; slave marriage; weddings

freedom: economic freedom in *Dred*, 36–37; fictional marriage associated with, 25, 41, 43–44, 54; free black womanhood, 58; imperfect freedom in *Garies*, 61–62; legalization of slave marriages, 1, 85; legal marriage associated with, 15, 49–51, 55, 85, 100, 105, 109; manumission by marriage, 29; postbellum racial identity and, 91–93, 100; as problem for marriage, 10. *See also* escape; free black marriage

Gardner, Eric, 108
Garies and Their Friends, The (Webb): black femininity in, 124–25n56; depiction of lawyers in, 112; Esther Ellis and Mr. Walters courtship, 47, 58–60; free black antebellum community in, 10–11; free black marriage as theme, 47–49; Garie conjugal/marital relationship, 50–56; mob violence in, 55–63; writing and reception of, 49, 52
Garnet, Henry Highland, 58
Gates, Henry Louis, 108
Genovese, Eugene E., 4
Gray, Annie Elizabeth, 10
Griggs, Sutton E., 89
Grimké, Angelina, 33, 69
Grimké, Sarah, 6, 32, 33
Guilllory, Monique, 24
Gutman, Herbert, 4, 128n9

Hamilton, Thomas, 65
Hammerton, James, 117n12
Harper, Frances E. W.: anti-amalgamation views of, 89; comparative studies of, 74–75, 127nn38–39; on coverture, 12–13, 64–65; critique of the women's movement, 71–72; as fiction writer, 68; as free black female public figure, 58; on free marriage, 63, 72–73, 76; as lecturer,

70–71, 74, 80; marriage of, 64, 71–72, 82; on single women, 64–66, 69–70, 77–78; on white women, 72, 73–74, 76. Works: "The Two Offers" (1859), 12–13, 64–66, 68–71, 78–80; "The Triumph of Freedom" (1860), 68; *Minnie's Sacrifice* (1869), 67, 69, 74, 76–77; *Sowing and Reaping* (1876–1877), 67, 69, 77–80; *Trial and Triumph* (1888–1889), 67, 69, 77; *Iola Leroy* (1892), 12, 67–69, 80–81, 109

Hartman, Saidya V., 52
Hedrick, Joan, 44
Hemings, Sally, 10, 115n35
Hodes, Martha, 4–5
Hoeller, Hildegard, 78

Jacobs, Harriet A., 7–8, 37, 57, 58, 120n24
James, Henry, 70
Jefferson, Thomas, 10, 115n35
Jones, Edward P., 107
Jones, Jacqueline, 78, 127n51
Joyner, Charles, 4

Kaplan, Amy, 61–62
Karcher, Carolyn L., 6
Kent, James, 43

law: *Colson v. Quander* (legitimation), 119n2; consent to marry, 1, 3; contractual status of marriage, 3, 114n10; depiction of lawyer characters, 111–12; "higher law" slave-marriage principle, 2–3, 31–33, 48, 52–53, 113n6; lawyers as fictional characters, 111–12; *Plessy v. Ferguson* Supreme Court ruling, 94–95, 97. *See also* coverture; legal marriage; property

Lee, Jarena, 58
legal marriage: as basis for coverture, 32–33; Blackstone definition of, 32–33; as commitment, 23, 93; domestic violence accommodated by, 119n11; feminist critique of, 2, 28, 32–34; freedom associated with, 15, 49–51, 55, 85, 100, 105, 109; management of citizenship and, 12; marriage as legal contract, 3; mar-

ried women's property acts, 33; nonlegal marital domains, 3; prohibition of mixed-race marriages, 85–89, 101–3; property as basis for, 22, 24, 25, 30; as racial affiliation, 53–63, 97–99, 100, 107; Reconstruction-era slave marriage, 11–12, 83–84, 91–93; selective legitimacy, 96; wealth as marriage obstacle, 47; wedding ceremony importance in, 9, 50; white vs. black marriages, 73–74, 78, 87. *See also* free black marriage; law; public sanction; separation/divorce; slave marriage; weddings

Lincoln, Abraham, 124n42

literacy, 17

Locke, John, 114n9

love (authentic love): authentic loyalty (Harry and Nina) in *Dred*, 37–39; Christianity as basis for, 9; compensation for imperfections by, 19–20; as democratic/egalitarian union, 24; forced separation and, 22, 28–30; marital fidelity as basis for, 7–8, 23, 29–30; personal freedom as basis for, 25–26; Reconstruction-era race laws and, 92–93; slave marriage as marriage ideal, 2–3, 6, 10, 16, 31, 41–42, 48; white love in mixed-race marriages, 101–2. *See also* sexuality

marriage. *See* coverture; free black marriage; legal marriage; love; marriages and conjugal relationships; slave marriage

marriages and conjugal relationships

—historical figures: Angelina Grimké and Theodore Weld, 69; Frances and Fenton Harper, 64, 71–72; Frank and Mary Webb, 49; Frederick and Anna Douglass, 15; Lucy Stone and Henry Blackwell, 118n64; Thomas Jefferson and Sally Hemings, 10, 115n35; William and Ellen Craft, 8–9, 28, 110; William W. Brown and Annie Elizabeth Gray, 10, 30; William W. Brown and Elizabeth Schooner, 10, 17, 18–21

—*The Bondwoman's Narrative* (Craft): Charlotte and William, 110–12

—"Cicely's Dream" (Chesnutt): Cicely and John, 103–4

—*Clotel* (Brown): Clotel-Horatio-Gertrude, 23–26, 50–51; Georgina and Carlton Peck, 26–28; Mary and George Green, 28–29; Mary Green and Mr. Devenant, 28–29

—*Dred* (Stowe): Fanny Peyton and George Russell, 45–46; Harry and Lisette, 35, 39–42, 111; Nina Gordon and Edward Clayton, 39, 43–45; Sue Peyton and John Cripps, 45–46

—*Garies and Their Friends, The* (Webb): Charlie Ellis and Emily Garie, 60–63; Clarence Garie and Emily Winston, 50–56, 61; Esther Ellis and Mr. Walters, 47, 58–60, 64, 124–25n56

—"Her Virginia Mammy" (Chesnutt): Clara Hohlfelder and John, 101–3; Mrs. Harper slave marriage, 102–3

—*Iola Leroy* (Harper): Aunt Katie and Uncle Daniel, 81; Aunt Linda and Uncle Daniel, 82; Iola Leroy and Dr. Gresham, 69, 127n39; Iola Leroy and Dr. Latimer, 80–82

—*The Marrow of Tradition* (Chesnutt): Cataret family (Olivia), 94–97, 104; Miller family (William), 94–97; Mr. Merkell and Julia Brown, 95–97

—"A Matter of Principle" (Chesnutt): Alice Clayton and Jack, 100–101

—*Minnie's Sacrifice* (Harper): Camilla La Croix, 76–77; Louis and Minnie, 69, 74, 76–77

—*Sowing and Reaping* (Harper): Belle Gordon and Paul Clifford, 69, 77–80; Jeanette Roland and Charles Romaine, 77–78

—*Trial and Triumph* (Harper): Annette, 69, 77

—"The Two Offers" (Harper): Janette Alston, 64–66, 69–70, 78–81; John Anderson, 79–80; Laura Lagrange, 64, 65–66, 69–71, 79

—*Uncle Tom's Cabin* (Stowe): George and Eliza Harris, 8–9, 10, 34, 110
—"Uncle Wellington's Wives" (Chesnutt): Uncle Wellington and Aunt Milly, 83–88, 93
—*What Answer?* (Dickinson): Francesca Ercildoune and Willie Surrey, 74–75
—"The Wife of His Youth" (Chesnutt): Mr. Ryder and Liza Jane, 88–91, 93, 97–100, 104; Mr. Ryder and Molly Dixon, 88–91, 93, 99–100, 106
Moore, Hannah, 44
Morrison, Toni, 6–7, 107
Moynihan, Daniel Patrick, 114n14

Nash, Gary, 122n8
National Woman Suffrage Association, 71
neo-slave narratives, 4–5

Page, Walter Hines, 91
Paine, Thomas, 27
passing: Clarence Garie in New York, 56, 62; George (*Clotel*) in Europe, 28; in Harper vs. Dickinson, 74; hidden racial ambiguity as marriage issue, 101–4; Miriam's grandson in *Minnie's Sacrifice*, 76. *See also* race
Penningroth, Dylan C., 37
performative historiographical mode, 4–5
Peterson, Carla L., 58
Pike, Mary Hayden Green, 73
Plessy v. Ferguson Supreme Court ruling, 94–95, 97
Prince, Nancy, 58
property: accumulation of freedom through, 36–37; as basis for legal marriage, 22, 24, 25, 30; free-black property as threat to white social order, 56; ironic property in *Dred*, 35–38, 45–46; wealth as marriage obstacle, 47. *See also* coverture; law
public sanction (in marriage): exposure of Brown/Schooner marital difficulties, 19–20; false affection in weddings, 7; free black marriage and, 11, 53–58; marriage as joining of families, 20; public sanction importance to marriage, 13–14, 20–21. *See also* legal marriage

Quincy, Edmund, 15

race: *Anglo-African Magazine* approach to, 65; Chesnutt "color line," 84–85, 87–88, 94–95, 105–6; Garie children as mixed-race whites, 50, 56; Harper critique of the women's movement, 71–72; intermarriage by light-skinned blacks, 80–81, 84; light-skinned female slave stereotype, 40; marriage as racial affiliation, 53–63, 97–99, 100, 107; middle-class "Blue Veins," 81, 84, 87, 88–91, 99–101; prohibition of mixed-race marriages, 85–89, 101–3; racial amalgamation theory, 89, 91–93, 124n42; racist opposition to black legal marriage, 55–63, 75; segregation, 94–95, 97; social equality at quadroon balls, 24; white vs. black marriages, 73–74, 78, 87. *See also* passing; Reconstruction era
racial uplift theory, 12–13, 86, 100
rape (sexual assault by slaveholders), 3, 7, 52, 57–58, 120n24
Reconstruction era: black suffrage movement, 75–76; legal marriage significance in, 11–12, 104–5; legitimation of slave marriages, 13, 84, 119n2; *Plessy v. Ferguson* Supreme Court ruling, 94–95, 97; postslavery slave community, 12–13; prohibition of mixed-race marriages, 85–89, 89–90, 101–3; racial loyalty as marriage factor, 100. *See also* free black marriage; race
Reid-Pharr, Robert, 124–25n56
Remond, Sarah Parker, 58
resistance: fictional alternatives to legal marriage, 8; to mob violence in *Garies*, 58–61; to Reconstruction-era legal marriage, 12; slave families as transgressive social entities, 35–38; slave marriage as, 3–4
Robbins, Hollis, 108

Rousseau, Jean-Jacques, 26–27
Ruffin, Thomas, 34

Sanchez-Eppler, Karen, 119n12
Schooner, Elizabeth, 10, 17, 18–21
Schureman, W. D. W., 73
Scott, Dred, 124n42
Sedgwick, Catherine Maria, 64
segregation, 94–95, 97
selective legitimacy, 96
separation/divorce: Brown-Schooner separation publicity, 19–20; divorce as private realm, 117n12; forced separation by slaveholders, 2, 8–9, 17–18, 21–22, 28–30, 110–11; legal non-recognition of slave marriage, 83; owner protection of slave marriage, 81; reuniting of broken families, 85. *See also* free black marriage; legal marriage; slave marriage
sexuality: sexual assault by slaveholders, 3, 7, 52, 57–58, 120n24; in slave marriage, 14, 40; slave-owner consensual sexuality, 36, 54, 57; symbolic incest in *Garies*, 60–63; white-woman/black-man sex, 4. *See also* love
single lifestyle, 64–66, 69–70, 77–78
slaveholders: acceptance of slave bigamy/ adultery, 22–23; dissolution of slave marriages by, 2, 8–9, 17–18, 21; forced marriage of slaves, 18, 21, 108–9; sexual assault by, 3, 7, 52, 57–58, 120n24; slave marriage as asset for, 2; slave-owner marriage, 10–11; views of slave marriage, 16–17, 73. *See also* slavery
slave marriage: overview, 1, 11; as concubinage, 31–32, 52; contractual status of, 3, 114n10; egalitarian relationships in, 8, 11, 21, 27–28, 32, 78, 127n51; as forced marriage, 18, 21, 108–9, 111–12; "happy ending" marriage narrative and, 29, 48, 61–63, 80–81, 87, 102, 109; "higher law" principle of, 2–3, 31–33, 48, 52–53, 113n6; historical treatment of, 120n19; impermanence of, 2, 9, 110–11; motivations for, 2, 3–4; as nonviolent resistance, 3–4; omission in fictional narrative, 9, 17; racial loyalty and, 100;

Reconstruction-era slave marriage, 12, 83–84, 100; religious condemnation of, 73; sentimental discourse and, 3, 113–14n7; as source of shame, 15–16. *See also* free black marriage; legal marriage; love; separation/divorce
slave-owner conjugal relations: Garie-Winston fictional marriage, 50–51; Harper depiction of, 80; historical accounts of, 120n24; legalization of, 54; mistress jealousy and, 37; Webb account of, 11. Examples: Clarence Garie and Emily Winston (*Garies*), 50–56; Horatio and Clotel (*Clotel*), 23–26, 50–51; Mary Green and Mr. Devenant (*Clotel*), 28–29; Thomas Jefferson and Sally Hemings, 10, 115n35. *See also* slavery
slavery: inner experience of, 98–99, 104–5, 114n14; postslavery slave community, 12–13; Ruffin decision effect on, 34; slave contentment in *Dred*, 41–42; slave families, 35–38. *See also* slaveholders; slave-owner conjugal relations
Sollors, Werner, 99
Southworth, E. D. E. N., 73
spinsterhood, 64
Stanley, Amy Dru, 97
Stanton, Elizabeth Cady, 65, 71, 76, 119n9
Stewart, Maria, 58
Still, William, 68
Stone, Lucy, 28, 118n64
Stowe, Harriet Beecher: antislavery themes in, 41–42; Crafts as model for, 8–9; critique of legal marriage, 33–34, 39–42, 48; critique of property, 36–39; sentimental discourse in, 113–14n7; on slave marriage as concubinage, 31–32; women's rights and, 42–44, 119n9, 119n11–12. Works: *Uncle Tom's Cabin* (1852), 8–10, 34, 44, 119n9; *Dred* (1856), see main entry *Dred*; *The Minister's Wooing* (1859), 10, 32; "The Woman Question" (1868), 119n11

Tate, Claudia, 11–12, 49, 74, 100
Tocqueville, Alexis de, 32

Tompkins, Jane, 113–14n7
Truth, Sojourner, 58

Voltaire, 27

Walker, David, 58
Warner, Michael, 20–21, 96
Warner, Susan, 73
Washington, Mary Helen, 77
Webb, Frank, 48–49, 89, 124n42. See also
   Garies and Their Friends, The
Webb, Mary E., 10, 49
weddings: as Craft escape component, 9;
   false affection in slaveholder weddings,
   7; ironic mirth in *Bondwoman* wedding, 109–10; love conquest of prejudice in *What Answer?* 75. *See also* free
   black marriage; legal marriage

Weinstein, Cindy, 48, 73–74
Weld, Theodore Dwight, 69
White, Deborah Gray, 4, 57
Whitney, Lisa, 34
Williams, Sherley Anne, 107
Wilson, Harriet E., 58
Wollstonecraft, Mary, 44, 114n9
women: feminist critique of marriage, 2,
   28, 32–34, 64–65, 67, 119n9, 119nn11–12;
   free black female public figures, 58–59;
   Harper critique of the women's move-
   ment, 71–72; Nina Gordon (*Dred*) as
   women's rights advocate, 42–43; resis-
   tance to mob violence by, 57–61; single
   lifestyle and, 64–66, 77–78
Wonham, Henry, 89
Woodhull, Victoria, 119n9

TESS CHAKKALAKAL is an
assistant professor of Africana studies
and English at Bowdoin College.

The University of Illinois Press
is a founding member of the
Association of American University Presses.

Composed in 10.5/13 Adobe Minion Pro
at the University of Illinois Press
Manufactured by Thomson-Shore, Inc.

University of Illinois Press
1325 South Oak Street
Champaign, IL 61820-6903
www.press.uillinois.edu